DUE DATE	BRODART	01/05	6.99

ne
rk
fer
ne
ib-
ist
en
his
zy
tu-
on
y's
ry
or
er-
ou

2/05

"I have no idea where I am," he said.

"I just drove off the side of the mountain. We were coming down."

"You were driving down the mountain?" the dispatcher asked.

"We were coming down. And I was braking. And it wouldn't stop," he said, the hysteria returning. "It wouldn't stop!" He started sobbing. "It wouldn't stop!"

"Calm down," the dispatcher said. "I need you to calm down so we can get you some help."

But he didn't calm down.

"Sir," she said, calmly but firmly, "I need you to take a deep breath. We need to get you some help."

But all he did was shout. "Rinette!" Rinette!" he cried. "It wouldn't stop! It wouldn't stop!"

St. Martin's True Crime Library Titles
by Michael Fleeman

"If I Die…"

The Stranger in My Bed

Laci

Over the Edge

Over the Edge

MICHAEL FLEEMAN

St. Martin's Paperbacks

OVER THE EDGE

ISBN: 0-312-98703-X
EAN: 80312-98703-9

Printed in the United States of America

St. Martin's Paperbacks edition / November 2004

10 9 8 7 6 5 4 3 2 1

Over the Edge

Chapter 1

In the stillness of the mountain night, a blue Ford F-150 pickup truck stopped at the end of the road, the headlights sweeping across the gate blocking off the parking lot to the Slide Mountain Ski Area. It was just before midnight on the last day of May 1998 and dirty patches of snow remained, soon to be washed away by the spring rains. The only lights came from the cab of the pickup and the stars. A man got out of the truck. He was in his forties, stocky, with bushy eyebrows. He wore blue jeans, a dress shirt, a jacket, canvas shoes, gloves and a green-and-white baseball cap with "Incline" written across the front. He lit a thin Cuban cigar and paced. He raised his voice and profanity punctured the night.

In time, the man got back into the truck and drove from the ski area, with the radio on, the window rolled down and the heater off. Heading down the 1950s-era road, rarely used in the skiing off-season, the man drove a few hundred feet to a broad, banking left turn, where the road was wide enough to pull over to the side, next to the guardrail that separated the pavement from the side of a cliff. From this precipice, there was a sweeping view of the Washoe Valley, some 3,000 feet below, where on this clear night the lights of Sparks and Washoe City twinkled to the right.

Next to the guardrail a windsock hung, limp. By day, this is a jumping-off place for hang-gliding enthusiasts, who leap from the edge past the guardrail and catch the updrafts created when the sun warms the valley floor. A skilled flier can ride these thermals all day, soaring thousands of feet, over the ledge, and land near the shores of Lake Tahoe.

Had the man steered the truck on the gentle left and gone past the turnout, he would have seen in the valley below the blazing blanket of lights of Reno. He never made it.

A tremendous crash shattered the mountain quiet. Metal slashed through metal, wood splintered, glass shattered, as the truck barreled through the guardrail and soared off into the vast nothing before striking the rocky slope 100 feet down, then tumbling. The camper shell went flying off as the truck cut a swath down the hill, scattering clothes and suitcases and paperback books and a pair of plastic cans that spewed gasoline.

The truck came to a thunderous halt 700 feet below the guardrail, lying upside down and facing uphill in the rocks and a clump of manzanita bushes.

Hundreds of feet back up the slope, the man lay on his stomach, clinging to a branch with one hand and his cellular phone with the other, screaming hysterically to the 911 operator, then shouting, "Rinette! Rinette!"

Below him, in the mangled remains of the overturned truck, dangling upside down from a seatbelt, was his wife.

Chapter 2

"Nevada Highway Patrol."

It was just after midnight at the Reno dispatch center. Michelle Lewis was working the graveyard shift, sitting in front of her two computer screens at the dispatch console. She wore two headsets, one delivering 911 calls into her right ear, the other transmitting dispatches from patrol cars and other emergency vehicles into her left ear. This night, Lewis was handling calls from the rural sections of Washoe County while her partner, Paula Ryssman, fielded calls in the urban areas in and around Reno.

In her right ear, her 911 ear, Lewis could hear a man panting uncontrollably.

"Sir, sir," Lewis said in a measured voice into her headset mouthpiece. "Calm down. Where are you?"

"I'm on the side of the mountain!"

"Sir, sir," she said. "I need you to calm down. Where are you?"

He panted. "Ski resort. My wife is in the car."

"Sir, where are you?"

"I'm on the side of the mountain."

"You're on the side of the mountain?" asked Lewis, exasperation creeping into her voice. Reno is surrounded by mountains. "What mountain is that? Sir, we need to get somebody out to help you. You need to tell me where you're at. I need you to take a couple of breaths and then tell me where you're at."

Her computer screen told her only that he was calling from a cellular phone. It didn't give her a location.

"I'm on the side of the mountain off the edge," he said. "My car went down the hill. My wife is in the car."

"OK, we'll get someone right out there," said Lewis. "You're on . . . Which mountain are you at?"

"Up by the ski resort."

"Up by the ski resort?"

"Yes, ma'am."

"OK, hang on the line." Lewis knew that cell phone reception worked only from one mountain with a ski area: Mount Rose, about 25 miles southwest of Reno. Cell phones didn't work from the other resorts in South Lake Tahoe or Heavenly Valley. "Sir, are you by Mount Rose?"

"Yes."

"How far from the ski resort are you?"

"It's the Slide Mountain area. It's not Mount Rose. It's Slide Mountain."

Slide Mountain—the Slide Side or East Bowl as locals call it—is on the eastern side of the Mount Rose–Ski Tahoe Resort and accessible by a different entrance from the main ski area, a distinction that got lost in the early hysteria, complicating the rescue operation.

By now, 12:20 a.m., Lewis had stood up and started pacing, dragging her headset cords behind her. She worked better on her feet. She stood over her partner, Ryssman, who scribbled down the information from the man and radioed highway patrol cars to respond to Mount Rose to look for a man who had gotten into an accident. Normally Lewis, with her two headsets, would handle both matters: the 911 call and the patrol car dispatch. But from the hysterical tone of the man, she knew this was going to be a difficult call, so she handed off the dispatch duties to Ryssman. Along with radioing the patrol cars, Ryssman phoned the Washoe County Sheriff's Department's substation in Incline, just over the summit from the Slide Mountain Ski Area.

"Hi, Incline," she said, "this is Paula from Nevada Highway Patrol. We have a subject on the line. He says that his wife—he's very hysterical—he says that his wife is inside the vehicle, the vehicle rolled off the side of the mountain up by the ski resort. The Mount Rose ski resort. Do you have someone up there?"

The deputy on night watch said, "The Mount Rose ski resort?"

"Yeah, that's the best that he's got," said Ryssman, who, in the transfer of information from Lewis, didn't get that the man was actually on the eastern, Slide Mountain side. "We've got him on the other line here, and he's just extremely hysterical."

"OK, what kind of vehicle is it?"

"I don't know. He said that the vehicle rolled off the side of the mountain and his wife's in it."

"All we know is that it's by the Mount Rose ski resort?" asked the sheriff.

"That's all I got so far. We do have him on the other line trying to get further."

On that other line, the man was groaning, "Ah, ahhh, ahhh," while Lewis was imploring him to "Calm down, calm down."

"I'm sliding down the hill," the man said. Then he shouted, "Rinette! Rinette!" before moaning into the phone.

Lewis tried to pinpoint the man's location. She asked, "How far down the mountain is the vehicle?"

"I can't even see it," he said, then again shouted, "Rinette! Rinette!"

Things were now happening all at once: Lewis on the line with the groaning man, Ryssman on the line with an increasingly frustrated sheriff's man, who asked again, "No description of the vehicle?"

"No description," said Ryssman.

"OK," the sheriff said, "what I'm going to do is, I'm going to send a deputy up from my end and try to contact Reno and have them send a deputy from Reno."

Ryssman then dispatched two highway patrol cars from Reno. That would allow for rescuers to come up both sides of the mountain on the Mount Rose Highway, deputies from Incline to the west, the highway patrol troopers from Reno to the east. There would now be at least four cars scouring the mountain. The burden rested with Michelle Lewis to get the man to calm down long enough to give them a better description of his location.

As the man moaned, Lewis said in a concerned, even tone, "Calm down. What kind of vehicle is it?"

He did calm down. "It's a Ford truck," he said.

"It's a what?" she asked. The phone reception suddenly had become fuzzy.

"A Ford truck."

"It's a truck?"

"Yes, ma'am."

"OK," said Lewis. She told Ryssman that it was a Ford that had crashed on Mount Rose. She returned her attention to the man. "OK," she told him, "we've got people on the way to you. Do you know how far from the ski resort you were?"

He only answered her with heavy breathing. "I didn't

hear you," he said, then he moaned, "Oh, oh, oh, oooooooh."

"Have you been injured?" Lewis asked.

"My ankle and my back."

"Your back?" This was a bad sign.

"Yes, ma'am," the man answered.

"OK," she said, with a now more serious tone. A person with an injured back must be handled with extreme care because of the risk of paralysis. "I want you to stay still. Are you still with the vehicle?"

"No," he said, "the vehicle is down the hill. I was thrown out. I'm sliding down the hill. I've got to hang on with one arm. I can't hang on. I'm sliding down the hill."

His voice raised in intensity, ending with an "Oh!" and then heaving sobs.

"You're what?" asked the dispatcher, but all he answered with was, "Ooooh, oooh."

"What's your name, hon?"

All she heard was moaning, more, "Uh, uh, oh, uh, uhhhhh, uhhh!"

"Stay with me," she pleaded.

"Uh, uhhh," he said, then gave out with a long groan followed by fast breathing.

"Stay with me," she said. "Take deep breaths. I don't want you hyperventilating."

Then the man shouted the woman's name again. "Rinette! Rinette! Rinette!"

Lewis tried to distract him from Rinette for a moment and refocus his attention on the accident, seeking more information to pass on to the sheriff and highway patrol officers now working their way up the dark, curving roads up each side of Mount Rose.

"Can you see the car from—"

But before she could finish her question, the man blurted out fragments of details from the crash. "It went down the hill. Way down the hill," he said. "Oh, God! Oh, God!" The heaving sobs came again, with a long "Ahhh-hhhh."

"Can you see the road from where you are?" she asked. She needed to know where he was. She was being pressed by the other dispatcher for a better location.

He moaned.

"Can you see the highway?" asked Lewis.

"No, ma'am," he said, then moaned something unintelligible.

"No, you can't see the highway?"

"No, ma'am."

"OK," she said, backing off. She said "OK" with a tender, concerned tone, like she was comforting a sick child. She didn't want to lose him.

He breathed heavily again, then cried.

So far, all Lewis could elicit from him was that he had crashed his Ford on the mountain, that he was thrown from the truck, that his wife had stayed inside the vehicle. The crash occurred somewhere near the Mount Rose ski resort. Lewis continued to feed what little information she had to her partner dispatcher, Ryssman. With the man complaining of back pain, the dispatchers now had to call for medical help. While the man continued to moan into the phone, Ryssman dialed paramedics.

"Hi, this is Paula from Nevada Highway Patrol," she said. "We've got a report of some sort of accident. We're landlined with the PR." PR is cop-speak for Person Reporting. "He's extremely hysterical. He's advising that his vehicle rolled off the side of the mountain and his wife's still in the vehicle."

"And where was this at?" asked the paramedic dispatcher.

"On Mount Rose, in the area of the Mount Rose ski area," said Ryssman.

"The ski area?"

"Right."

"Where's he at right now?" asked the paramedic dispatcher.

"I don't know. He's calling from his cell phone."

"Oh, he's on his cell phone?"

"Yes, he's calling from his cell phone."

"So when we get up there, he'll be able to flag us down, then?"

"Hopefully," said Ryssman, though her voice didn't carry much hope. "He's extremely hysterical. I don't know if he's going to be able to make it until then. He's just— that's the most we've got."

"We can't get his cell number from him?" asked the paramedic dispatcher.

"He's on the line," said Ryssman. "We barely got his location. If we can get his cell phone for you, we'll get it."

"If you can, go ahead and give us a call back. We're on our way."

While still on the phone with the man, Highway Patrol Dispatcher Lewis could overhear her frustrated partner talking to the paramedics. Lewis again asked the man, "Do you know how far off the road you are?"

"I have no idea where I am," he said, a note of calm now creeping into his voice. "I just drove off the side of the mountain. We were coming down."

"You were driving down the mountain?" she asked.

"We were coming down. And I was braking. And it wouldn't stop," he said, the hysteria returning. "It wouldn't stop!" He started sobbing. "It wouldn't stop!"

"Calm down," Lewis said. "I need you to calm down so we can get you some help."

But he didn't calm down.

"It wouldn't stop!" he cried, his voice slurred by the

sobs. "It wouldn't stop! It wouldn't stop! It wouldn't stop!"

"Sir," she said, calmly but firmly, "I need you take a deep breath. We need to get you some help."

But all he did was shout the name again. "Rinette! Rinette!" he cried. "It wouldn't stop!" he repeated, then more sobs.

"Sir," she said over the sounds of his crying, "I want you to listen to me."

"Why didn't it stop?" he cried, then shouted, "Rinette! Rinette! It wouldn't stop."

"Sir, calm down. I need you to help me," said Lewis. "We've got officers and ambulances on the way to you, but I need you to help me." Then she remembered what the paramedic dispatcher had wanted. "What is your cell phone number that you're calling me on?"

The man composed himself long enough to give the phone number, which Lewis jotted down and relayed to Ryssman.

"OK, calm down," Lewis said. "You're doing fine. Now tell me what color your truck is."

"It's blue," the man said, sniffling.

"It's blue. OK. You're doing good. Calm down. Calm down. Stay with me. What's your name, hon?"

He only answered with a weak, "Uh, uh, uh," but his crying subsided.

The man had given the highway patrol precious little with which to work. A frustrated Ryssman told the dispatcher at the sheriff's station in Reno, "We've got a subject landline advising that his vehicle rolled off the mountain. He's on Mount Rose. Probably east of the Mount Rose ski area. But he's not sure. But he said his vehicle rolled off the mountain and his wife's inside of it. Do you guys have anybody in that area?"

"Are you guys responding?" asked the sheriff dispatcher.

"We're responding. Our closest unit is en route from Reno."

"You need Hasty Team?"—the volunteer rescue team that works with the sheriff's department.

"I have no idea," said Ryssman. "We're still on the line with him. We're trying to get as much as we can out of him, but he's hysterical. He's on the verge of hyperventilating. And I've got medical en route. Incline's going to check their side."

"What would be the closest cross?"

"Mount Rose ski area, in that area."

"And he's actually on the highway?"

"As far as we know. As far as we know he's on the highway," she said, annoyance creeping into her voice. "He's calling from his cell phone. How he got his cell phone out of the vehicle when his vehicle rolled, I don't know."

"We got a call in," said the sheriff's dispatcher. "We got it from Incline."

"Great," said Ryssman.

To try to narrow down the man's location, Dispatcher Lewis asked him if he could see the road.

"No," he said. His voice was much calmer.

"You can't see the road?" Lewis said. "OK, what I want you to do is, I want you to listen for the sirens."

"Yes, ma'am."

"And we're going to have a bunch of lights, and I need you to tell me when they get close to you so we can find you."

"Yes, ma'am."

"OK?"

"Yes, ma'am."

Lewis told Ryssman, "He can't see the road from where he's at," then again told the man, "We have a bunch of people on the way to you."

"OK," he said, now with no trace of panic.

"You're not going to hear them just yet, but it will be soon. OK?"

The calm didn't last.

The man began to sob. "Why didn't it stop?"

"It's OK," said Lewis, trying to maintain the precious calm in an attempt to pinpoint his location on the mountain. "We've got help. It's OK. Calm down."

"It wouldn't stop," he repeated, and the sobs returned. "It wouldn't stop. Oh, God."

"OK, stay with me. We've got a bunch of people on the way to see you. I can't understand you on your cell phone very well," she said, trying to keep him talking and distract him from his plight. "How long ago did you leave the ski resort?"

"Ten minutes ago."

"About ten minutes ago?" said Lewis.

Ryssman then asked Lewis if the man was still in the truck and whether he could flag down the troopers looking for him. Lewis told Ryssman, "He says he was thrown out of it. He's out of the vehicle," while in Lewis' headset she could hear the man lament, "Why me? Why me? Why not my wife? Why me? Why not my wife?" and start sobbing again.

"OK, stay with me. Stay with me," Lewis pleaded, wanting to keep him talking. "Were you headed back to Reno?"

"We were up talking. We were talking for a while." His voice was broken by the sobs. "We were talking," he said, then muttered something about "the lights" and then the hysterical mantra, "It wouldn't stop. It wouldn't stop."

"OK, calm down," said Lewis. "You were headed back down to Reno from the ski resort?"

"We were up on the top."

"You were what?"

"We were up by the top of the hill at Slide Mountain Ski Area."

"You were up by Slide Mountain?"

"Yes, ma'am."

She thought she heard the man say that he and his wife were headed down Mount Rose, about ten minutes from the Slide Mountain Ski Area, presumably on the one major road down the hill—Mount Rose Highway. But this was only a presumption. There were a lot of roads on the mountain, particularly in the residential areas down the mountain, and he could be anywhere.

By now, a third person, Trooper Steven Pagni, had come into the dispatch office to help with the calls, the first coming from a woman with a chirpy voice saying, "This is REMSA." REMSA wasn't the woman's name; it's the acronym for the Regional Emergency Medical Services Authority, a private company that provides ambulance services, both trucks and a Care Flight helicopter.

"Hello, REMSA," Pagni replied.

"The caller you still have on line from Mount Rose Highway?" she said.

"Yeah, dispatch is on with them," Pagni said. "They had me answer this line."

"Yeah," she said, her voice full of a friendliness that belied the situation. REMSA gets 100 calls a day, and for people like these dispatchers, this is an ordinary night's work. "Could you ask him if he thinks his wife is trapped?"

The man shouted over to Lewis and Ryssman, "Does he think his wife is trapped?"

Ryssman replied, "He thinks she's dead."

Pagni told the REMSA dispatcher, "He thinks she's dead."

"He thinks she's dead?"

"Yes," he said.

"There's not movement in the car?" asked the REMSA dispatcher. "You guys headed up that way?"

"He was leaving the ski resort heading towards Reno when he went off the road," said Pagni.

"He wasn't able to tell you if she was conscious or breathing?"

"No, he was real shook up," he said. "Dispatch was having a heck of a time just trying to get him to calm down so they could find out what was going on."

"He didn't have an answer for you when you asked if she was trapped?" asked the REMSA dispatcher.

"Hold on a sec," he said, then asked the other dispatchers one more time, "He said he thinks she's dead?"

"About ten minutes ago," one of the dispatchers replied.

"Conscious or breathing?" he asked.

"He's not in the car," the dispatcher said. "He's been thrown out of it."

Pagni told the REMSA dispatcher, "She's in the car. He's been thrown out of it. He's away from the vehicle."

"Thrown out of the car?" she asked.

"He was, not her. He doesn't know what her condition is."

"OK, we're on our way. We're going to send Care Flight." Care Flight is the part of the REMSA service that sends a McDonnell Douglas 900 Explorer helicopter with a nurse and paramedic on board to remote areas to respond to emergencies.

"Hold on," said Pagni, then asked the dispatcher, "Do you think Care Flight is necessary?"

Sending a Care Flight helicopter is an expensive decision—for the victim, anyway. Since REMSA is a private company, the person being transported must pick up the cost of the rescue.

"Probably," the dispatcher told him. "He's away from the roadway. He can't see the road."

Pagni then told the REMSA dispatcher, "OK, do that."

Now, the search for the man would take to the air, while those on the ground still didn't know exactly where to look. The Incline sheriff's substation dispatcher called the Nevada Highway Patrol, asking, "Any update on this vehicle, where we might start looking for it?"

"He said that he was leaving the Mount Rose ski area, headed towards Reno," said Pagni. "Unknown how far he went down."

"OK. One female occupant in the vehicle?" asked the sheriff's dispatcher.

"As far as we know. He's saying that he was inside the vehicle, and then he was thrown out and his wife was still in the vehicle when this happened."

"OK, have you still got him on landline?"

"Still have him on landline."

"OK, very good," and the sheriff's dispatcher hung up.

On that landline, the man was beginning to show signs of hyperventilating again. Michelle Lewis continued to pepper him with questions to get a better idea of where he was in relation to the Slide Mountain Ski Area.

"You're at the ski area?" she asked.

"Yes," he said, "the gate is closed. You can't go in there."

"You couldn't get into it?"

"We're about one hundred yards away from it, looking at the view, of the lights."

The information seemed to be changing. First he'd said ten minutes away from the ski resort, now he said 100 yards. She knew there was an access road to the Slide Mountain side, but that road was usually closed to all but emergency vehicles at the turnoff on Mount Rose

Highway. That meant he had to be off the main highway somewhere. The units were all over the mountain by now, but couldn't find him. She needed to keep him on the line.

"OK," she said. "You're doing good. Now, stay with me."

He answered with a sob.

"I need your help," she said. "Now, we need to find you." She asked the other dispatcher, "Where are the units at?" Ryssman told her the patrol cars were on Mount Rose Highway near the summit. "OK," Lewis told the man, "listen to me now, there are units on the highway that you're on. I need you to start listening for them, OK?"

"OK," he said.

Lewis relayed to Ryssman and Pagni, who were talking to paramedics and the sheriff's office, that the man may not be able to see the units and that he would be going by the sounds of the sirens because he was off the highway.

"OK," Lewis told the man, "I want you to start listening for them. They're on the mountain."

"OK," he said.

"And they're going to start heading up to you. I don't want you moving around, though. You said your back is injured. So I don't want you moving around."

"OK, I'm just holding on."

"OK, you're doing fine. You're doing just fine. Now, tell me what your name is again, hon?"

"It's Peter."

Chapter 3

The lights reminded him of home, of the lights he used to see from his father's house in the foothills, where Peter Bergna would sit and watch the glow from the high-tech factories in San Jose and Cupertino that sprouted where the groves of plum trees once stood. Peter would remember the lights and think of romance. He would think of Rinette.

The house that Peter Bergna's father, Louis P. Bergna, built in Saratoga, California, south of San Francisco, loomed over the Santa Clara Valley in the way that Louis Bergna lorded over Santa Clara County for nearly thirty years. As the county's highest-ranking law-enforcement officer, Lou Bergna, first elected as district attorney in 1955, commanded both power and respect. Six times he went to the polls, six times he won unopposed. None dared take on Lou Bergna, and none saw any reason to. His reputation as an administrator, lawyer and citizen was spotless. Any time an old friend from legal circles approached him for a favor on a case, he'd scribble a note to an underling: "No deals—LPB." He would gain national recognition by serving as president of the National District Attorneys Association and he was once offered a judgeship, but turned it down. As a litigator, Lou Bergna was the stuff of legend. His most famous case—the murder trial of Dr. Geza de Kaplany, charged with the butcher-knife mutilation and acid-melting of a wife he suspected of being unfaithful—featured a scene right out of *Perry Mason*. For his defense, the Hungarian anesthesiologist claimed to have had a split personality. But Bergna tracked down a former lover of Kaplany's from Germany to refute that. Bergna brought the witness into court, and won a conviction.

His abilities and integrity were matched only by his modesty. He was born in San Francisco, and at age 5 he suffered polio. For the rest of his life, he walked with a limp and his right arm was barely usable. He would shake hands with his left hand, twisting it around to accommodate a person's right hand. He remained active, in and out of the office. He used to like to ride around on a tractor on his estate and he played golf almost to his final day. Through inheritance and thrifty living, he built—on his government prosecutor's salary—a $4 million net worth, enough to build a beautiful house on the hill, from which his son would watch the lights in the valley below.

Lou Bergna's record of public service would have been unblemished but for something that occurred at the end of his career, in 1982. It began with Bergna announcing his retirement and endorsing, as his hand-picked successor, an assistant district attorney named Leo Himmelsbach. Then, about a week before the election, a damaging story about Himmelsbach appeared in the local paper, the *San Jose Mercury News*. Quoting confidential sources, the story contained information that had to have come from personnel documents in the DA's office.

An angry Louis Bergna, in his final act as elected prosecutor, called a press conference to announce that Himmelsbach's election opponent, Julius Finkelstein, another prosecutor, had been suspended on suspicion of being part of the news leak. Finkelstein, who would lose the election, went to court to challenge the suspension. Although Finkelstein and another prosecutor would acknowledge going through some résumés on a secretary's desk, Finkelstein always maintained he wasn't responsible for the *Mercury News* leak and that his suspension was unfair, damaging his career and reputation and causing him emotional distress.

The legal fight would drag on for nearly a decade. After a state attorney general's probe failed to uncover any conclusive evidence of wrongdoing by Finkelstein, a jury in San Francisco found in 1991 that the charge against him wasn't true and awarded him $1.2 million. The county abandoned the fight and agreed, in a settlement, to resolve the matter by paying more than $1 million to Finkelstein and nearly that much to his legal team.

Louis P. Bergna's going-away present to the taxpayers of the county he'd served for so long was a legal tab of $2 million.

Still, this long, bitter and ultimately expensive fight would be but a footnote, not even mentioned in the glowing newspaper tributes when he died.

To grow up in the Bergna house was to be constantly reminded of greatness. The brag-walls of Louis Bergna's home office were covered with the framed and mounted plaques and certificates from the groups that revered him over the decades. He worked with the Red Cross and with disadvantaged kids. A Boy Scout as a youth, Bergna was awarded a distinguished Eagle Scout commendation for professional excellence when he grew up and went into law.

Being raised by Louis and Pat Bergna meant that truth, justice and punishment weren't abstractions, but the family business. By all accounts, their second-oldest child, Peter, found his place under the wing of an Eagle Scout.

Like his siblings, David, Louanne and Maryellen, Peter was adopted. As he grew up and attended the local public schools, Peter was neither a great standout, nor did he do anything to cause embarrassment to his father. His father was strict, but Peter "never rebelled," said friend Rick Martin. "He didn't drink. He didn't smoke. He was pretty straight and narrow in his own lifestyle." He made the football team at Saratoga High School, but was hardly a star. He went to college in the northwest, at Seattle Pacific College, a small Christian school, majoring in education. He became a big fan of soccer—but only a fan. He never played, though he would coach.

In the summer of 1973, Martin was just out of high school when he met Peter at a kids' summer camp in Canada where they both worked as counselors. At the time, Peter was attending Seattle Pacific. "Peter was always a very gregarious, fun-loving guy, very outgoing," recalled Martin. "Most everyone liked him. Kids liked him. He was a lot of fun." By coincidence, their paths would cross again four years later when they both were working as dorm supervisors at Harker Academy, a private school in San Jose. While there, Peter developed an interest in antiques—or, as Martin recalled it, an interest in antiques-buying. On the weekends, they would go to garage sales and flea markets picking up old furniture—tables, dressers and the like—that Peter would restore and resell for a profit. "Even before he bought them he had people in mind he would sell them to," recalled Martin. "He loved wheeling and dealing. He was good at it. And he loved doing it." So much so that he would buy and sell antiques on behalf of others and let them keep the profits. Bergna decided that he would try to make this his living.

Having studied education in college, he had much to learn about the antiques trade—it was one thing to work garage sales, another to compete in the world of professional dealers. He boned up on the antique business by poring over books and studying auction sales the way others would follow sports teams. During his self-training, he moved to the upscale Sierra Nevada community of Incline Village, on the Nevada shore of Lake Tahoe, to work in an appliance store. Peter had no love of washers and dryers—antiques were his passion—and in 1986, after acquiring his license, he was hired as a freelance appraiser for the prestigious San Francisco–based auction house Butterfields.

As a generalist appraiser, Bergna would look over a piece of furniture, a vase or a tin wind-up toy and tell the owner how much he thought it would fetch at auction—preferably an auction handled by Butterfields. The items could be anything from family heirlooms to items somebody had found tucked away at a garage sale and suspected might be worth something. A large amount of business dealt with trust estate officers who needed to sell the belongings of somebody who had died. Working out of his home in Incline Village, he handled West Coast appraisals for Butterfields and quickly earned the respect of colleagues and customers. Peter possessed all the qualities of a first-rate appraiser: the vast knowledge of the history and characteristics of items to assess not only their value but to root out fakes, and a good knowledge of the antique market. Just as important, he deftly walked the appraiser's tightrope, valuing items attractively enough to convince people to sell them at a Butterfields auction—where the company fetched a 17.5 percent cut—but not so high as to be unrealistic, setting up the seller for disappointment if the item gets a lower price. In an industry that relies on repeat business, Peter knew how to treat people well. He remembered their names and gave them the time of day, no matter what the size of the appraisal. He never forgot his manners; even under the most stressful situations, he would remember to say his "Yes, sirs" and "Yes, ma'ams." Always hoping to find that hidden treasure, he was eager to travel across the West—California, Nevada, Oregon, Washington—meeting with clients, going to appraisal seminars, discussing business with estates. He ran up the odometer on the truck he would drive—always a Ford pickup, with a shell, to haul the objects around if need be.

He would rise at Butterfields from a contract appraiser to a regional representative by 1996, earning about $100,000 a year, and becoming the first regional rep to score a consignment of more than $1 million: a collection of old slot machines and antique weapons from the legendary Harolds Club casino, which operated from 1935 to 1970. He never seemed to tire of that thrill of the hunt he'd discovered back in college. "He liked finding something at a garage sale for twenty dollars and selling it at an auction in San Francisco for two hundred dollars," Adelaide Gramanz, one of his employees, would later recall in court. He once found a table in Reno for $700 and sold it in San Francisco for $20,000. Another time he discovered several paintings for a few thousand dollars each and sold them for about $20,000 apiece. Of course, it didn't always work out that profitably, and his enthusiasm could get the best of him. A Reno casino had wine in storage for a long time and approached Peter about buying it. "He got very excited because a lot of them were really big French names which he recognized," Gramanz said. "But he's not really an expert at wine." He spent a small fortune, only to discover—too late—that the wine had been improperly kept in a storage locker exposed to the harsh Reno summers. The fancy French wine had turned into bad French vinegar and Peter, she said, took "a big loss."

Off the job, his loyalty and friendship were well known, that Eagle Scout ethic from his father evident. An old friend from Saratoga, Gary Espinosa, owed an incredible debt of gratitude to Peter. In the early 1980s, Espinosa's daughter suffered Tourette syndrome, and nothing the doctors did seemed to work. Espinosa shared his frustrations with Bergna. "He stopped over and saw how we were suffering, and believe me, we were suffering," Espinosa would later say in court. "Any person who has a child with Tourette syndrome suffers, let me tell you. All families do." But Peter did more than sympathize. He contacted a friend in the pharmaceutical business who knew about medication for Tourette's that had been approved in England but not yet in the United States. Using his connections, Peter helped place the daughter on the medication on a two-year trial basis and, Espinosa would emotionally recall, "We started getting our daughter back. Peter did what all the professionals couldn't."

Peter was so giving, so friendly, that some people didn't know what to think. He enjoyed being around people, particularly young people, and was always described as friendly and gregarious, if at times a little too much so. Peter was what they would call a close-talker, and those who didn't know him well could misinterpret his intentions.

"I would characterize it more as a little touchy-feely," Gramanz would recall. "You know, he gives people hugs that, you know, maybe he's not that close to." Mark Steven Sampson, a soccer coach from Southern California and a longtime friend of Bergna's, said that Bergna didn't just like being around people—he seemed to need it. "As long as I have known him, he's wanted to surround himself with people," Sampson would recall, "and I think being lonely is one of his greatest fears."

A marriage came and went in the early 1980s—he never talked about it to his friends. As far as those around him were concerned, his true love was always a petite former farm girl with a bubbly personality to match Peter's outgoing nature.

Peter would remember those nights in Saratoga, when he sat on the hill and watched the lights below, Rinette at his side.

Chapter 4

"Peter?" Michelle Lewis repeated his name. "Peter, you're doing really good. I want you to calm down so we can get you help. You're doing just fine."

The Nevada Highway Patrol dispatcher had been on the phone with this man for more than fifteen minutes, an eternity in 911 rescue operations. It was approaching 12:30 a.m. on the first day of June 1998. There were highway patrol cruisers, sheriff's cars and a Care Flight helicopter all looking for him on Mount Rose, and still, all they knew about his location was that he was somewhere off the road, clinging to branches and rocks, his back and head hurting, sobbing, hyperventilating and screaming for a woman named Rinette, whom he believed was still in his truck, somewhere farther down the mountain in the darkness.

The dispatcher asked Peter if there was anything the rescuers should look for to help find him.

"There's a big hole," Peter told her. "There's a big hole in the, in the, in the fence."

"There's a big hole in the fence?" she asked.

"Yeah, where we went over the edge."

"Where your truck went through it?"

"Yes."

"OK," she said, and now another clue—another sign-post. She had been able to keep him on the line and slowly, very slowly, she was getting the information she needed.

She told the other dispatcher, Paula Ryssman, "He went through a fence."

"A fence?" asked Ryssman.

Lewis wasn't certain. She asked Peter, "Is it a fence or a guardrail?"

"Guardrail, yes," he said.

"It's a guardrail?" asked Lewis.

"Yes, ma'am."

Lewis told her partner Ryssman, "It's a guardrail. He went off the guardrail."

Then, to Peter, she said, "Take it easy, Peter. You went off the guardrail? You went through the guardrail?"

"Yes, ma'am."

"Were you on a curve? Were you coming on a curve when you wrecked?"

"I don't remember."

"You don't remember, OK," Lewis replied, then told Ryssman, "He doesn't remember if he was on a curve when he went through a guardrail." Then, back to Peter, "OK, you're doing just fine, Peter. You were headed down the hill from the ski resort?"

"Right, It's real close to the entrance of the ski area."

"You were close to the entrance of the ski area?"

"Yes, ma'am, at the top."

"OK, and you're on Mount Rose Highway?"

"No."

Armed with this new information—near the ski area but off the roadway—dispatcher Ryssman dialed the Washoe County sheriff's substation in Incline Village, and said, "Washoe County, the RP is advising that he's *not* on the highway. He went through a fence. He's off the side of the highway on a hill. He said he went through a fence or a guardrail, or something like that."

"My units have just cleared the summit and are heading down," the sheriff's dispatcher said. "You need to contact Washoe"—the station at the bottom of the mountain— "and let them know because they got units coming up."

"Thanks," she said, and dialed that station.

"Washoe County," a female voice answered.

"Hi, Washoe, this is Paula from Highway Patrol," said Paula Ryssman.

"Hey," she said. Another night at the dispatch desk.

"Our RP is advising . . ." Ryssman stopped herself and asked Lewis, who was still on the phone with Peter, "If you could get his cell phone from him, Michelle"—then returned to the Washoe County dispatcher. "RP is advising that he went through a guardrail, he's not on the highway. He's off the side of the mountain somewhere, so they're going to need some sort of infrared lights or night lights or something like that to look for him if you guys have that."

"OK, he went through a guardrail?" asked the sheriff's dispatcher.

"He said he went through a guardrail," said Ryssman.

"He's on the mountain somewhere?"

"Right. He said he was ejected from the vehicle. His wife is still in the vehicle."

"OK, thanks."

"Sure, bye."

By now, Peter was lucid enough to start giving better directions to Dispatcher Lewis. He was telling her, "If you're at Mount Rose Highway, and you turn onto the road that takes you to the ski area . . ."

"OK."

". . . we're about, I don't know, three, four, five hundred yards from the entrance. I can see the mountain where we turned around, where people ski, on Slide Mountain."

"OK, so you went past the entrance of the ski resort?"

"No, the gate right at the top of the hill is closed."

"The gate said it was closed, OK."

"Right."

"Good, good, OK, that's helpful," said Lewis. "And you were only a couple miles away from that entrance there?"

"No, a couple hundred yards."

"Couple hundred yards," Lewis repeated, then relayed to dispatcher Ryssman, "He's only a couple hundred yards from the entrance to the ski resort." Lewis went back to Peter. "OK, you're doing just fine. We've got a bunch of units up there looking for you, so I still want you to listen for them. Do you have any idea how far off the road you are?"

Only silence. Had she suddenly lost him?

"Are you with me, Pete?"

His voice came back. "I have no idea, ma'am."

"OK."

"I just know," he said, "that we turned around up by Slide Mountain Ski Area. I hear a siren now."

A rescuer was finally close.

"OK, you're doing good," said Lewis, her voice getting a little more excited. "You can hear them? Can you hear the sirens?"

"Far away."

"They're far away?" Lewis asked, then she told Ryssman, "He can hear them but they're far away." Back to Peter, Lewis said, "OK, let me know if they're getting closer."

"OK," he said.

"How are you feeling, Pete? Are you all right?"

"My head hurts, my back hurts, and my ankle hurts bad."

"OK, I want you to stay still. You're talking just fine. Is your head OK?"

"Yes."

"Yeah?"

"The top of my head hurts."

"Your head hurts?"

"I don't feel any blood."

"OK, you're doing just fine. I want you to keep talking to me, OK?"

"I'm listening."

"OK, you're doing just fine. Can you still hear the sirens?"

"No, ma'am."

"No?" she said, puzzled. There weren't too many places for cars to get to atop the mountain near the ski resort. Where could he be? "OK, you said you couldn't see your truck from where you are?" asked Lewis.

"No, ma'am. It was way down the hill."

"OK, no problem. Could you tell after you crashed if the lights on your truck were still on?"

"I can't look."

"You couldn't? OK, that's all right. That's fine. OK, can you hear them now? Can you hear them, Peter?"

"Let me listen," he said. There was a pause. "No."

Lewis told Ryssman, "He can't hear them." Then she said to Peter, "I want you to stay with me, now."

With the rescue vehicle somewhere in the area, then suddenly gone, Lewis tried to figure out a way to narrow down Peter's location. He was near the entrance to the Slide Mountain Ski Area, on the side of the mountain off the road, with a ripped-out guardrail as an obvious marker, but still they couldn't find him. Even in the middle of the night, this shouldn't be that difficult. Lewis also worried about Peter's physical and mental health; it couldn't be good, complaining of both back and head pain and suffering what seemed to be obvious emotional distress.

"Were you coming down the hill from Tahoe?" Lewis asked. Maybe he was on the other side, the western side, of the ski resort entrance.

"I picked her up at the airport," he said.

"You picked her up, where?"

"At the airport. And we came up Mount Rose," he said. That was likely the Reno/Tahoe International Airport, and the road he took up would have been the Mount Rose Highway, the main road up the mountain from the Washoe Valley up the eastern side. "And we made a left on the Slide Mountain, where you go skiing. That's that little road."

"OK, OK. You're doing just fine," she said. "They're up there looking. They're up there looking for you."

The dispatcher tried to sort this all out. It would appear he had gone off the main highway, Mount Rose Highway—Highway 431—but off an access road to the ski area.

She told Ryssman, "He's on Slide Mountain road, not Mount Rose Highway. They were coming down the 431 to go to Slide Mountain, the road has a gate and the gate is closed, so they continued going. I'm assuming the access road has a gate?" The gate was still confusing her. How could he be on the access road if the access road was blocked by a gate?

Lewis asked the man, "Peter, you still with me?"

"I'm here."

"OK. Can you see the ski resort from where you're at?"

"I could. I can't now. I'm down the side of the hill."

"OK, you're down the side of the hill. OK, that's fine."

So he was on that access road to the other side of the ski area.

"There has to be a big hole coming right through the guardrail," he repeated.

"OK, you went through the guardrail. Are there a lot of trees around you or anything we can look at to find you?"

"There are no trees around me."

"No trees?" she asked.

"We're real close to where people ski at Slide Mountain," he said.

"OK, you're doing just fine. You're doing fine."

"I hear them again."

Sirens.

"You hear them again? OK," she said, then told Ryssman, "Let them know he can hear them again." Then back to Peter, "OK, stay with me. Let me know if they get louder."

"They're getting a little louder now," he said. He was starting to breathe heavily again.

"OK, calm down. Can you hear them still?"

"Yes."

"Yes, you can hear them? OK, stay with me. I don't want you moving around. You said your back is hurt?"

"Yes, lower back."

"OK, I don't want you moving around. You just stay still. We're going to find you. Are they getting louder now?"

"I don't hear them now."

"You don't hear them now?" she asked, befuddled. This was getting perplexing. It was as if they were driving right by him, yet not seeing him or the hole in the guardrail.

"No," he said.

Dispatcher Ryssman, on the line with the other authorities, asked Lewis if the man could hear the sirens still. "What about now?"

"OK," Lewis asked Peter, "can you hear them now?"

"No, ma'am."

"No," Lewis relayed to Ryssman, who then said over the phone, "That's negative." Lewis didn't want Peter to get discouraged by this puzzling problem. "OK, we're going to keep doing this until we can track you down, but we're going by the sound of their sirens, OK?" she said. "OK, stay with me, Pete."

"If you go up the ski area, on Slide Mountain, it's right up there," he said. There was a new tone to his voice: impatience. "I turned around at the top of the mountain and told my wife how beautiful it looked, and you couldn't get up there because the gate was closed."

Lewis hoped this would help find him. She said to Ryssman, "He's a couple hundred feet from an entrance to the ski resort where there's a gate and it says it is closed." Then she said to Peter, "OK, stay with me, Pete. Can you hear them now?"

"No."

"OK, we're still up there looking for you. We're still with you."

Indeed they were. By now the Washoe County sheriff's dispatcher had called the highway patrol dispatcher center and, speaking with Officer Steven Rani, still handling the overflow calls, asked, "Any luck from Mount Rose?"

"No, we're up by Slide access road and we still haven't found him."

"OK, thank you," said the sheriff's dispatcher, and hung up.

Then the woman from the ambulance service called back. "Hi, it's REMSA again," she said in her friendly voice.

"Hi, REMSA," said Pagni.

"You guys still on line with that guy?" the REMSA dispatcher asked.

"We're still on line. He says his back's hurt."

"OK. Where exactly is he?"

"We don't know. We're up by the Slide access road and he said that he can't hear the siren. So, so far we're not sure where he's at, but it's somewhere between Sky Tavern"—a restaurant down the hill on the highway—"and the Slide access road. That's only a guess now. We don't know where. But our units are at the Slide access road and he couldn't hear the siren anymore."

Overhearing this, Dispatcher Lewis, still on the phone with Peter, told Pagni, "Tell them to look for a large chunk of guardrail gone."

Peter continued to tell Lewis he was on this access road to the ski area. "It enters Slide Mountain Ski Area. That's what I'm on, I think."

"Are you actually on that road, do you know? You said it was closed?" she asked. Earlier, she thought she'd heard him say the access road was blocked off by a gate at the main highway. In the off-season, that road is often accessible only by emergency vehicles.

"The entrance to the ski area is closed," he said. "The road's open."

"OK, the entrance to the ski area is closed, but the road is open. Did you take the access road to Slide Mountain?"

"Yes, ma'am."

Now it finally made sense. The access road itself was blocked off at some point near the ski area, not right at the intersection with the main highway.

"He's on the access road to Slide," Lewis relayed to Pagni. Then to Peter, "OK, let me know if you can hear them."

But Peter was thinking about something else.

"Rinette! Rinette!" he shouted.

"Can you hear them?" Lewis said, trying to get him to focus on the sirens. "Peter, can you hear them?"

"My wife is in the car. Oh, God."

"Can you hear them?"

"I can't hear them, I can't see anything."

"Keep listening for them, please. We're up on the access road now," she said, then repeated the information to the others working the phones. "He's at the access road," she told Ryssman, "but didn't make it all the way to the ski resort. They were coming down the access road." Ryssman told Lewis the location of the highway patrol cars on the mountain.

"OK, now we're up by the access road," Lewis told Peter, "so I need you to listen for them."

"No, I'm at the end," he said.

"You're at the end?" she asked.

"The end of the road," Peter said. "By the top."

The rescuers had to be close, but for some reason the man couldn't hear the sirens. Pagni told the woman from REMSA, "He can't see any lights [of the pickup]. He got thrown out. He's out in the trees. And he can't even see the vehicle."

"Oh, he's still in the trees?" the REMSA woman asked.

He actually wasn't. He had said he wasn't in the trees, but the information, in all the confusion, didn't get relayed to Pagni, who said, "Yeah."

"Not even on the road?" asked the REMSA woman.

"No, he's down in the trees," said Pagni. "He can't see any lights or anything."

"OK, we'll see if, when Care Flight gets up there, maybe they can start shining their light."

"Yeah, that's what I was hoping. You got radio contact with them, right?"

"Yeah," she said, "but we don't have any idea . . . Maybe . . . What exact area?" She wanted some idea of where to shine this light.

"Well . . ."

"Or how far down from Mount Rose, like how many minutes, does he recall?"

"No. First he thought he was ten minutes from the ski area, then he thought he was two hundred yards from the ski area. And he's not in good shape. Tell Care Flight, if they can spot it with their light, to check off the road on the south."

"On the south side?"

"On the south side, because they were coming downhill."

"OK."

"Between Sky Tavern and the Slide access road."

"I'll let them know that."

"We don't have radio contact with them, so call us back if they find him."

"OK," she said.

"Thanks," he said.

"Bye."

"Bye."

Still on the phone with the stranded Peter, Dispatcher Lewis could only listen to him lament.

"My wife needs more help than I am."

"We've got people on the way," she told them. "We've got a whole bunch of people on the way to help you."

"I don't know where she is."

"We're going to help you. I need you to keep listening for them."

He began to moan again. "Oh, God. Oh, God."

"Stay with me, Pete," she said. "You're doing fine. I need your help. You're doing good. You're doing just fine."

Then, finally a break.

"Is there a helicopter?" Peter asked.

"Yes!" she said, excitedly. It was the Care Flight helicopter. REMSA's McDonnell Douglas 900 Explorer with two turbine-powered engines and a powerful spotlight. "Can you see a helicopter?"

"I'm on my stomach. I can't move my hips."

"Can you see it?"

"No, ma'am. But I thought I heard it, though."

"You thought you heard it? OK, we have ambulances and helicopters out looking for you. So you're doing good. That's helping us get to you."

"I hear a helicopter," he said again.

"You hear a helicopter?"

"Yes."

The dispatcher said to the others, "He can hear the helicopter."

"It's not very loud," Peter said.

"What?" she asked. His cell phone connection was suddenly fuzzy.

"It's not loud."

"It's getting loud?" she asked, the reception returning. She struggled to understand him.

"It's not loud at all."

"It's *not* loud?"

"No, ma'am."

"OK, now, they're going to start shining lights down on you to try to find you."

"Yes."

"As soon as one of them hits you, I need to know that."

"Yes, ma'am."

Pagni quickly dialed REMSA. The pace intensified in the dispatch room, the voices grew more urgent, with everybody talking at the same time.

"Hello, REMSA," Pagni asked when he heard a woman's voice, "are you the one that's been calling me?"

"Yeah," came the familiar chirpy voice.

"It's Highway Patrol. Hey, yeah, is Care Flight in the area?"

"They are. Let me check their location. Hold on."

While she was checking, Peter told Lewis, "It's very loud now."

"It's very loud now?" she asked. "The helicopter is?"

"You're very close," Peter said.

Lewis relayed to Pagni, "He said, 'You're very close.'"

"Right there," Peter said.

"The helicopter or the sirens?"

"I see lights. I hear them right there," Peter said, then he shouted again, "Rinette! Rinette! Rinette!"

"You're doing good. Good, Pete. Good, Pete. Stay on the phone with me. Stay on top of it," she told Peter, then said to the other dispatchers, "I can hear the sirens through the phone." Then back to Peter, "You're doing good, Pete. You're doing just fine."

Pagni told the REMSA dispatcher, "The sirens are on top of him. They're up on the Slide access road."

They had the location: On the access road, near the closed-down entrance to the ski area, about a half-mile off Mount Rose Highway. Two highway patrol troopers had arrived on the scene and advised the dispatchers that there was plenty of room for the Care Flight helicopter to land.

Through the phone, Dispatcher Lewis, on the line with Peter, could hear him shouting to somebody, "Right there! Right there! My wife! My wife is down at the bottom of the hill! My wife's at the bottom of the hill! She's still in the car!"

"Are you doing OK?" came a voice.

It was one of the troopers, John Schilling.

"Yes," Peter said. "I was thrown out. I had my window open and I was thrown out."

"Tell them you're going to hang up," the trooper said.

"OK," he said.

Lewis, overhearing this, said, "Go ahead, Pete, go ahead."

"Thank you," he told her.

"You're welcome," she said.

Then, the last thing she heard before hanging up on the stranded man, was the voice of Schilling shouting to somebody else, "We're right here!"

When it was all over, Michelle Lewis took a deep breath and looked at her partner, Paula Ryssman. They both had the same puzzled look. "How on God's green Earth," Michelle asked her partner, "could he have managed to have a cell phone on him?"

Chapter 5

Nevada Highway Patrol Trooper Rick McLellan got the call from dispatch at 12:20 a.m. reporting that a man had called 911 from his cellular phone to say that his truck had gone through a guardrail off Mount Rose about ten minutes from the entrance to the Slide Mountain Ski Area. McLellan was in Reno, but with siren blaring and lights flashing on his Crown Victoria—and nobody on the roads at that hour—he made good time reaching the 8,200-foot summit of Mount Rose, arriving in just fifteen minutes. The problem was that he saw no sign of an accident anywhere on the side of Highway 431, Mount Rose Highway—not ten minutes from the ski area, not twenty minutes, nothing. What he did see was a Washoe County sheriff's deputy at the summit, who had raced up from the other side of the mountain from the Incline Village substation and who also couldn't find the crash scene.

McLellan turned around and started back down the mountain, asking dispatchers to ask the man if he could hear the trooper's siren. McLellan was told the man couldn't. The trooper drove a couple miles, then saw a small road off the highway. He turned onto the road—a poorly maintained, unlighted ribbon of pavement on the side of the Sierra Nevadas with a guardrail on one side with a sweeping view of the valley below, and the steep incline of the rocky mountainside on the other. Snowplow markers lined both sides of the roadway.

Not far from the turnoff, on his left, McLellan located what he hadn't seen on the main road: a ripped-out section of metal guardrail at what appeared to be a scenic turnout area. Illuminated by his headlights, the metal railing was bent back exposing a gaping hole big enough for a car to go through. Next to the hole was a windsock. A few hundred yards farther up the road, just around the bend, was the Slide Mountain Ski Area's parking lot, closed off from the road by a barricade.

McLellan pulled his patrol car to a stop in the turnout next to the hole, got out and walked to the precipice, guiding his way with his Maglite. It was a clear night, about 60 degrees, and he felt no chill through his short-sleeved blue uniform. Peering over the edge of the precipice he could make out the figure of a person lying down, a few dozen yards down the steep hill. He called and a man replied, "Right here! Right here!" The man shouted up that he had been thrown out of his car and his wife was at the bottom of the hill, still in the car.

McLellan was just about to work his way down the mountainside when his eye caught something on the side of the road next to the guardrail. It was a white-and-green baseball cap with "Incline" written on it. McLellan thought it looked out of place, and wondered how it got there.

"Down here!" the man shouted, and McLellan left the hat where it was. Carefully, he stepped off the edge of the mountain and went down the side, his boots giving him just enough traction against the loose rocks. He could see the man below him. Beyond the man was only darkness. McLellan estimated he trudged about eighty feet down the hillside before he got to the man, who was lying on his side, his head resting on his cell phone. He was surrounded by shrubs and rocks. The man was middle-aged, white, with dark hair, bushy eyebrows and no obvious signs of injury. He wore jeans and a jacket, but none of it appeared to be torn or even dirty, save for the dirt on the man's rear.

The trooper told the man to hang up on the 911 dispatcher, then asked him if he was OK.

"I can't move my legs, but I am OK," the man said. "Go find my wife. She's still in the vehicle." He told the trooper that his vehicle had tumbled farther down the hill.

Meanwhile, up at the turnout, a second highway patrol trooper, John Schilling, had arrived, parked his patrol car next to McLellan's, and was now making his way down the hillside. Like McLellan, Schilling had trouble finding the location. He, too, had run into a Washoe County sheriff's deputy coming down the hill as Schilling went up, neither knowing just where to go. The message from the dispatchers was that the accident had occurred off the side of the main highway. But Schilling had often skied on Mount Rose and knew there was a back entrance to Slide Mountain, accessible by a little road off Mount Rose Highway. He told the dispatcher to ask the person on the cell phone if it was possibly on the Slide Mountain ski area instead of Mount Rose Highway. Schilling got a call back that it possibly was. He headed that way, made a left turn and, as McLellan had done moments before, drove about a mile up the access road until he saw the hole in the guardrail and McLellan's cruiser parked next to it.

Schilling parked his car to the left of McLellan's in the turnout and kept his headlights on. He got out of the car and saw the big gap in the guardrail. He also saw a hole in the ground where one of the support posts had been, the vehicle having crashed through with enough force not only to rip apart the railing but also to uproot the support post. He, too, saw the hat on the ground with "Incline" written on it.

Schilling made particular note of these facts because he was a trained accident reconstructionist. Once the victim or victims were found, and sent out for medical treatment, if it was needed, it would likely fall to him to figure out from the tangled guardrail, fence-post hole and other clues what exactly had happened to make the vehicle sail off the mountain. As he stood at the gap in the railing, the Care Flight helicopter swooped over with deafening noise from its twin-turbine engines. It shined a spotlight on the hillside, presumably where the accident victim and McLellan were.

Wearing his short-sleeved summer uniform and shining his Maglite down the hill, he could see McLellan's flashlight beam and the figure of the trooper standing next to the prostrate man. McLellan yelled up that he had found somebody, and Schilling went down the steep incline, struggling to keep his balance. The ground was covered in something slick and stinky—oil or gas—that got on his pants and hands. It took him five minutes to reach the man and trooper, and he paused to catch his breath as McLellan told him about another victim farther down the hill where the vehicle had plummeted. McLellan then left Schilling with the man and ventured down the mountain.

The man complained of back pain and said he couldn't move his leg—normally serious complaints, possible signs of a spinal injury—but the complaints conflicted with what Schilling was seeing. As a daily witness to the havoc wreaked on human bodies by car accidents, Schilling thought that the man appeared in remarkable condition for somebody who had just been thrown from a truck that went off a cliff. The man had no major injuries that the trooper could see—no blood, for instance, or obvious broken bones. He wasn't even that dirty.

Just then, Schilling was joined by two sheriff's deputies who stumbled down the slope. Schilling told them to stay with the man so he could hook up with McLellan in looking for the truck, and as the trooper turned around, one of the deputies slipped on the loose rock and crashed into him, sending them both rolling down the mountain another dozen feet. They got up, brushed themselves off, and the sheriff's deputy went back up the hill to attend to the man while Schilling made his way downhill to find the truck. He didn't fall again, but the going was rough. He followed the swath cut through the rocks and bushes by the truck, passing debris—clothes and papers and auto parts—as well as a camper shell.

About 700 feet down the hill, lying in a clump of manzanita, was the wreckage of a pickup truck, now illuminated by the spotlights of the Care Flight helicopter that roared overhead. The truck lay upside down, facing uphill in the opposite direction that it had come, with its headlights broken out. The crash had crumpled the cab, with the roof crushed down almost to the headrest of the seat. Trooper McLellan was already there. As Schilling arrived, the two men squinted against the helicopter spotlight. McLellan radioed dispatch to ask Care Flight to "turn the damn light off," and shortly after that the helicopter cut the beam.

The woman was still in the crushed cab. She dangled upside down, still partially strapped in the seatbelt that was wrapped only around one of her arms. The driver's-side airbag had deployed and lay limp, but the airbag in front of the woman hadn't opened. Prying open the disfigured door and pushing aside debris, McLellan reached into the upside-down cab as far as he could and pressed his fingers against the woman's neck looking for a pulse. He felt nothing. He checked her wrist. Again no pulse. It was a long reach and he wasn't certain he was able to get the best position on her neck or wrist so the troopers decided to try to get her out of the cab for a better examination. They pried open the door some more, then, with Schilling's utility knife, cut away the seatbelt and pulled the woman out of the vehicle and laid her on the ground.

Schilling shined his Maglite on her. They saw her ravaged face and body and knew she was dead. Another check of the pulse confirmed it.

Care Flight still hovered overhead. Schilling signaled to the crew that their services weren't needed by making a slashing motion across his neck, the accepted signal meaning "patient not salvageable."

Back up the hill, paramedic Jeff Sambrano and partner Dave England of the Northern Lake Tahoe Fire Protection District were attending to the man. They had arrived at the turnout on the Slide Mountain access road shortly after the troopers and sheriff's deputies did, and by now this normally lonely and deserted area looked like a nighttime law-enforcement convention, the night aglow with emergency lights from the patrol cars and fire engines. Radios crackled and uniformed personnel swarmed. By now, a safety line had been set up by members of the Nevada Division of Forestry, with ropes and pulleys affixed to the railing and lines running down the hill. In his yellow firefighter pants, blue T-shirt and suspenders and a flashlight dangling from a metal ring on his belt, Sambrano put on a pair of surgical gloves, then, with his partner, carefully shimmied down the hill holding on to the safety rope.

About eighty feet down, they found the male crash victim half-reclined in the dirt. He seemed calm, and to Sambrano's trained eye—he had responded to hundreds of car crashes—in remarkably good physical condition. Still, Sambrano made the routine physical checks of the "ABCs" as rescuers call them: airway, breathing and circulation—pulse. All signs were OK. The man's airway was unblocked and he was breathing normally. The pulse, checked at the wrist, was within the normal range. Sambrano then sought to determine the man's level of consciousness by asking the usual questions:

"What is your name?"

"Peter," the man replied.

"What state are you in?"

"Nevada."

"What year is it?"

"1998."

"What happened?"

"I was in a vehicle that lost control and got thrown from the vehicle."

The brain seemed to be operating fine. In fact, as his first impression had indicated, this man named Peter appeared to have, miraculously, escaped any serious injury at all. Sambrano was surprised and puzzled, and continued to check for injuries that perhaps he couldn't see. It didn't make sense for somebody to have emerged from an ejection with so little injury. He touched and poked the man's body from head to toe searching for broken bones. He asked Peter to take a deep breath while he palpated the stomach. He examined the man's pelvis, legs and arms again. He gave him a grip test to see if there was any neurological damage, asking him to squeeze Sambrano's gloved hand. Then he had Peter push and pull on the feet against the force of the hand. The paramedic then examined for signs of shock—pale, sweaty skin; increased heart rate; increased breathing. Each test came up negative for injury. The man had total feeling and control of his extremities, no broken bones and no pain to indicate internal injury. The only problems were some ankle pain and some vague lower back pain.

As he would reflect on that examination years later, Sambrano found it all very strange. "Generally people that are ejected don't survive, and the ones that do survive sustain major injury, either orthopedically through spinal fractures or major pelvic fracture or chest injuries," he would recall, "or they sustain major head injuries or soft tissue injuries." This man didn't have so much as a scratch from broken glass.

But as Sambrano well knew, only so much information can be gleaned from an external examination, and the complaints of back pain could signal serious internal injuries that couldn't be determined in the field. And so the man named Peter was gingerly placed by emergency workers into a lightweight but strong sled-like device called a Stokes stretcher, and, with the use of the ropes and pulleys, dragged up the steep hill to the pull-out. Nearby, the Care Flight helicopter had landed in the parking lot of the Slide Mountain Ski Area and was awaiting the man's transport to the hospital.

The helicopter, with a nurse and an EMT on board, had left the helipad at the Washoe Medical Center in Reno at 12:34 a.m. and searched the slopes of Mount Rose for about ten minutes before spotting the man on the slope. When the trooper made the slashing motion across his neck, the helicopter pilot landed the craft in the parking lot a little after 1 a.m. to transport the male victim to the hospital. It took about a half-hour to strap the man into the gurney and drag him up the hill. Flight nurse Phyllis Tejeda and Emergency Medical Technician Mark Wilson stood on the rim and offered to go down and help, but were told by a firefighter, "Wait there and we'll bring him up. He's pretty stable."

When the rescuers got the man to the top of the hill, he was again put through the ABC test, this time by Tejeda, and again it was determined that there were no obstructions to the airway, no problems breathing and total consciousness. Tejeda asked the man his name, the date and the name of the President of the United States, and all of his responses indicated a clear mind. She checked his pulse; it was strong and regular, but a little fast. She checked his blood pressure: 210 over 98, slightly elevated—normal is about 120—but hardly dangerous, showing no sign of any internal bleeding. As Sambrano had determined before, there were also no signs of shock. The stethoscope to the man's chest detected no sounds of fluid in the lungs. The man wiggled his toes, so there was no sign of paralysis. Everything was at, or close to, normal. Still, as a precaution, the man was hooked up to an IV in case medications needed to be administered, and was carried into the helicopter.

As he was loaded in, he kept saying, "My wife. My wife. My wife. I think she's dead."

Although he appeared in distress, this was actually a good sign, medically, because it meant he was alert enough to speak and describe any pain he might be having. Tejeda asked the man to tell her how the accident had happened. He told her he had been driving down the hill, lost control, and hit the brakes, but the brakes didn't work, sending the vehicle off the cliff. She asked him if he'd had his seatbelt on—the seatbelt can cause a particular kind of injury, and she wanted to look for that. He said that he hadn't been wearing it.

"Were you ejected?" she asked him.

"Yes," he said.

"Did you lose consciousness?"

"No."

She checked for the kinds of injuries usually found in a traffic accident in which somebody is ejected: trauma to the head, chest, pelvis, neck or spine. She found nothing. She asked him where it hurt most, and he said his ankle. She found swelling and figured it may have been sprained or broken.

But while his body was intact, his emotions were in tatters. He soon became hysterical and again cried, "My wife, my wife, my wife, I think she's dead."

Over and over he said this, in between sobbing sounds, which, in light of the night's events, would not be surprising, except for one thing.

He shed no tears.

From a medical standpoint, this was cause for some concern, for crying without tears could be a sign of dehydration or shock. But this is a problem seen almost exclusively in children, not adults, and Tejeda was perplexed by his dry sobs. Maybe he had a tear duct problem that predated the accident, she thought. Nothing she could do about that now.

All she was faced with were a couple of relatively minor problems. For the ankle injury, she injected morphine into his IV to deaden the pain. She couldn't do anything about the dry eyes, but for the emotional hysterics she gave him a sedative called Versed, a cousin of Valium, to lower the blood pressure, which dropped from 210 to 160. It also eased the breathing, brought relaxation and had a short, but very real amnesiac effect; he wouldn't remember anything for about ten or twenty minutes after the drug was given, meaning that much of the Care Flight experience would be lost from his memory.

In the end, Care Flight nurse Tejeda determined he was a "stable transport." And while he might be suffering a hidden injury, she thought, as the helicopter neared the bright lights of Reno's twenty-four-hour casinos, this was one very lucky man—if luck had anything to do with it.

"Something," she thought, "is not right here."

He was unloaded from the helicopter and wheeled into the emergency room of Washoe Medical Center, where his sweatshirt was cut away and his dress shirt, sweatshirt and part of his jacket were thrown into the bio-waste bin. Nurses also took off his gloves and belt and placed him on a gurney in the middle of the emergency room. While there, a trooper spoke to him briefly and had him provide blood and urine samples for routine analysis in a traffic accident. He agreed without complaint. In all the confusion, it was lost as to who actually first told him about Rinette's fate—it was probably the trooper—but as the evening wore on, it was clear he knew.

At one point, after he spoke with the trooper, he asked if he could make a call, and was handed a cordless phone. One of the ER nurses, Jeanine Moorhead, heard him sobbing into the phone and telling somebody named Bill, in a desperate voice, "Oh, oh, it's terrible, it's horrible. She's dead." And yet, it was an odd scene to Moorhead because, although the man appeared inconsolable and made sobbing sounds, there were no tears. In Moorhead's opinion, there wasn't even any emotion in the face—just in the voice.

Chapter 6

On Mount Rose, at the crash site, Trooper John Schilling was gasping. It had taken him just five minutes to go down the hillside, but more than a half-hour to get back up, and he was bushed. When he got back up to the turnout, he found the area a bustle of activity—troopers, deputies, firefighters, volunteers from the Hasty Team: it seemed every emergency person on duty in Washoe County had responded to this accident, and that wasn't necessarily a good thing. Taking a sip of water from a bottle somebody handed him, he scanned the crowd for Trooper Rick McLellan, wanting to confer with him about the evidence at the scene—or, more accurately, what evidence hadn't been driven on, walked over and kicked around. As a crash investigator, Schilling would have preferred to have secured the scene to preserve the evidence. It was a little late for that, both up on the turnout, which was by now a parking lot for emergency vehicles, and for the hillside, where, he would say later, "everything that could be trampled had been trampled." In addition to him and

McLellan, several sheriff's deputies and other rescuers had shimmied down the mountain, right on top of the path of the truck and all the debris that had been strewn. He found McLellan and they tracked down a highway patrol photographer to take pictures of the roadway and the broken guardrail.

What seemed odd was not so much what Schilling found, but what he didn't find. There were no black marks in the roadway indicating a skid from slamming on the brakes, or a yaw mark from sliding tires during a sharp turn. In fact, there was no sharp turn to make. The turnout was only a few hundred feet down from the barrier to the ski area—the truck couldn't have picked up too much speed even if the man were gunning it—and the turnout where the truck had gone through the guardrail was located on a wide curve that was banked, or "super-elevated," in highway-design lingo, toward the mountain. There was plenty of room to turn left and avoid the cliff, even if the truck were going fast. To Schilling, it looked like the truck had gone straight into the guardrail, which meant it would have had to have made a sharp *right* turn on a curve that turned to the left. He asked himself, How did the truck go through like that? "This," he said to McLellan, "is a little weird."

Despite his concerns about the evidence, Schilling would ultimately add his boot prints to the investigation scene again, going back down the hill to the truck. It seemed that because of the darkness, some of the others sent down to retrieve the body simply couldn't find the vehicle. So Schilling went back down the hill for the second time that night, found the truck, and placed a light beacon on top so everybody else would know where to go. He then sat there awaiting a call from the coroner. Finally, the coroner asked if Schilling could bring the body up, so up the body went, yanked by ropes, in an ascent that took about an hour. The body was placed in a blue coroner's bag and laid on the roadway, awaiting pickup for the morgue.

By now, the sun was starting to rise on Monday, June 1, 1998, and the crowd at the crash site had been joined by one more lawman. Detective James Beltron of the Washoe County Sheriff's Department had been sent to the scene to help determine what had happened. Beltron joined Schilling and the two surveyed the crash scene, with Beltron now seeing what Schilling had seen: nothing—no skid marks, no yaw marks, no brake or transmission fluid, nothing that would suggest a cause of the crash.

By now, deputies were hauling up some of the debris from the hillside, including two red plastic gas cans. Also located was the green-and-white baseball cap with "Incline" written on it, though it had been moved by somebody from its original location on the side of the roadway in front of the guardrail and placed atop one of the wooden support posts on the railing. About 100 yards up the road from the turnout, at the gated entrance to the Slide Mountain ski area, Beltron found what looked like women's shoe marks in the dirt. He wondered if they belonged to the female victim, and why she would have been walking around outside the truck in the middle of the night. For that matter, Beltron wondered why the two were up on this lonely stretch of roadway to begin with.

As Beltron was walking the scene, a big car drove up, a Cadillac or a Lincoln as he recalled it, and in the front passenger seat was the dark-haired man with bushy eyebrows. By now, Beltron and Schilling knew the man's name: Peter Bergna, age 45, of 800 Geraldine Lane in Incline Village, only a few miles away from the crash site. They had gotten the name by running a check on the truck's upside-down license plate, a personalized plate that read, "FIFA."

The dead woman was identified as his wife, Rinette Riella-Bergna, age 49, of the same address.

The last time anybody had seen Peter Bergna he was being placed in a Care Flight helicopter on a stretcher complaining about back pain and screaming about his wife. When the man was driven up in the big car and signaled to Schilling, the trooper couldn't believe his eyes. Schilling wouldn't have been surprised if the man were hospitalized for months with internal injuries and even paralysis. Instead, Bergna was back on the mountain, and wanted to talk to Schilling. Bergna got out of the car and walked over to him, the only sign of problems being a limp. "I'm thinking, What is this?" recalled Schilling. "Mr. Incapacitated who can't move his legs walks over and wants to have a short conversation?"

They had that short conversation. Bergna had something he wanted to ask about. To Schilling's surprise, it wasn't anything about Bergna's wife—who still lay only a few feet away in a blue body bag. Bergna wanted to know if anybody had found his fanny pack. Schilling told him that he hadn't seen it, but would keep looking.

And then Bergna was driven away. He never asked about Rinette.

Yet another time that day, Schilling thought, This is awfully weird.

Beltron, who had overheard all of this, had another thought. It was time to have a longer talk with Peter Bergna.

Chapter 7

It would not be the warmest of receptions. "I just want you to know," a woman said to the four officers who had come to Bergna's chalet-style house, "that since you're taking Peter to be questioned, that I just gave him some medication."

"Are you a doctor?" Detective James Beltron asked her. The woman was taken aback. "No," she said.

"Well, why are you giving him medication?" Beltron asked.

"Because," the woman said, "it's on this sheet that he should be given this medication."

The woman, Adelaide Gramanz, was deeply concerned about Peter Bergna. Four officers had come to the house to pick him up and that, she thought, was excessive. She wanted them to know that whatever they were doing with him, that he had just taken medication for pain for his injured ankle. Peter, she felt, was already dazed and disoriented, and the medication might make things worse.

The house was buzzing with people like Gramanz, concerned friends and colleagues who would later say that Peter was anything but the man whom Trooper Schilling found so strange by returning to the crash scene with no apparent concern for his dead wife. "He looked like he'd been in an accident," said Peter's friend and neighbor, Allan Walker. "He was lying on the couch with his head down. His leg was wrapped. He had crutches near him. He just looked sad. He looked beat up. He was just lying there. Peter appeared to be hurt. Peter appeared to be in pain, physically and mentally. He cried. We cried together. We hugged. We held hands. I mean, this was a new experience for all of us. I didn't know how to act. Peter would be physically there and he wouldn't say anything. He'd be staring off somewhere, and I wouldn't know where Peter was. Peter was not Peter. Peter was with Rinette. Peter was with his— I don't know where Peter was."

Walker and his wife had been called early in the morning by a nurse telling them that their friend Peter had been in an accident and that his wife, also a dear friend, had been killed. The call left the Walkers stunned. They stared at each other, not knowing what to say. When it finally sank in, they went next door to see if there was anything they could do.

By 10 a.m., people were serving food and calling anybody whom they thought Peter knew to tell them about the crash. Into this home came the four lawmen: Sheriff's Detective James Beltron, evidence recovery man Deputy Jay Straits and their boss, Sergeant Dave Butko. Joining them was the first man on the scene, Highway Patrol Trooper Rick McLellan. While Gramanz would describe the show of force as excessive and their manners as rude, the officers would recall it differently, saying they'd tried to be as professional and sympathetic as possible, but also knew they had to speak with Bergna quickly—and by himself.

After they knocked and were let into the house, they went into the living room where they found Bergna seated on a sofa, surrounded by people. The officers introduced themselves and Beltron asked Bergna how he was doing.

"OK," he answered.

Beltron explained that they were investigating the crash and asked, "Would you like to go down to the station to speak to us?" Beltron wanted to get Bergna away from the hubbub at the house and into the quiet, controlled surroundings of a police station where the interview could be recorded.

"Yes," he said. Bergna's tone was cooperative.

Beltron asked Bergna if he still had the clothes he was wearing the night before, and Bergna pointed to a white bag near the front door. Bergna got up and hobbled off on crutches. Some of his friends then suggested that he should wait and get some rest before speaking with police, but he told them, "I'm going to go no matter what. I feel it's my duty."

On the way out, Straits picked up the white bag of clothes.

They caravanned to the Washoe County Sheriff's Department substation in Incline Village, just a couple of miles away, Butko driving his Ford Explorer with Bergna and Beltron in the back seats, Strait driving his unmarked car and McLellan driving his patrol car. They led Bergna through the lower-level entrance of the two-story building into a small office used by the substation's two detectives. There were a pair of desks pushed together, some file cabinets, and a large window which had a view through the trees of Lake Tahoe. The officers inspected Bergna's injuries, and Beltron, as the rescuers had before him, took note of how minor the wounds were—the bum ankle that had either been broken or sprained and an abrasion to the head that was so slight that Beltron considered it only a little worse than a carpet burn. Otherwise, this man who said he had been ejected from a truck onto the rocky mountainside appeared the model of good health.

Bergna took a seat. A tape-recorder was turned on. He gave the officers the basics: spelling of first and last name, date of birth (12-2-52), Social Security number, address (800 Geraldine, Incline Village) and phone number. Beltron also had Bergna confirm that he was aware the interview was being taped.

"And where do you currently work, sir?" asked Beltron.

"Um, I'm self-employed."

"Who do you work for?"

"Butterfield and Butterfield."

"OK, and what is that?"

"They're an international auction and appraisal company."

He said he had been there for eleven years.

He also gave the number of the cell phone he'd used to call for help.

Beltron announced for the tape that Trooper McLellan, Deputy Straits and Sergeant Butko were also in the room.

It was McLellan who began the questioning in earnest. "You're more than welcome to pull your chair up a little bit," he told Bergna. "The first thing I'd like to say is, I'm sorry for the accident that occurred tonight—for what's happened. What actually happened? We weren't there, so, you know, we got to sit down and figure out what happened. So if you could just tell it . . ."

It was a wide-open question and it got a long, rambling response that began with something that had nothing to do with what had happened.

"I'll back up a couple hours just so you know my wife is the president of Nevada Pharmacy Association," he said, "and she's also a tour director and she has been six weeks touring Italy, so she got home last night for the first time."

And then, in his first breath of the narrative, Bergna told the officers that he and his pharmacist wife had driven up to the mountain on her first night back from a European tour to look at the lights—and to talk about their marriage.

He told the officers, "I'm a lonely guy."

Chapter 8

Rinette Riella was 38 years old when a friend introduced her to Peter Bergna, then 35, in 1987. A devout Catholic, she was smart, vivacious and gregarious. It seemed, to all around them, a perfect match, and they were married within months, settling into a life of God, good friends and long vacations. She was a pharmacist and he was an art and antiques appraiser, and between them they made a very good living of some $200,000 a year. This allowed them to live comfortably in a half-million-dollar house in the pines not far from Lake Tahoe in one of the most exclusive hamlets in Nevada: Incline Village, with its beachfront mansions, mountain chalets, private beaches, golf courses, good weather (300 days of sunshine a year, the locals boast), classy casino–hotels and 8,000 of the friendliest—and in many cases, richest—people you'd ever want to meet.

She grew up on the family's dairy farm outside Manteca, California, in the San Joaquin Valley. The farm had about 120 Holstein cows, on a ranch that her grandfather bought in 1927, later expanded in the mid-50s by property her parents purchased. Rinette grew up with two younger brothers, Jack and Rick, and had a half-brother—her father's son by a previous marriage—who lived with a grandmother in San Francisco. Although the only girl sibling, Rinette "did her share" around the farm, Jack, a year younger than Rinette, would later tell the *Reno Gazette-Journal*. "She wasn't one who thought she was too good to do anything." Thirteen years older than Richard, she basically raised her youngest brother while their mother and father worked.

She attended Manteca High School, graduating in 1967, and left home—though not far—to attend the University of California, Davis. She graduated with honors in 1971 and had her sights set on going to medical school to become a pediatrician, but changed her mind and studied pharmacy at the University of the Pacific in Stockton, fifteen miles from Manteca, living at home for the three years of her study. After doing internships, she moved to Incline Village and plunged herself into her two passions—work and travel. She had family in northern Italy and had an affinity for Europe and its people.

Rinette and Peter lived in a house filled with Peter's antiques and art and a cellar full of Peter's wines, some worth more than $200 a bottle. In the basement was Peter's office, where employee Adelaide Gramanz worked. They would do what people in Incline Village do, their lives very much revolving around the community, the schools and the church. Peter coached soccer at the local high school, while Rinette sang in the Catholic church choir, tended to her garden—her specialties were tulips and half-barrels—and put in long hours working her way up to becoming director of pharmacy at Tahoe Forest Hospital in Truckee and at Carson Tahoe Hospital in Carson City. She would also do consulting work for a private company that worked with pharmacies.

They traveled extensively in North America and Europe, and opened their beautiful home to friends and neighbors. The marriage, brother Rick Riella would observe, "seemed somewhat normal." It was, indeed, a quiet, comfortable life.

And that, Peter would complain, was the problem. Peter wanted children, and Rinette did not, and Peter wanted Rinette coming home every night, and Rinette did not. The strain reached its peak when Rinette decided to give up her pharmacy career, take a 50 percent pay cut, and work as a tour guide, spending weeks on end away from Peter.

Peter told the officers: "One of our favorite spots was to go up to Slide Mountain and to sit by ourselves from time to time and look over the valley and think, like people do, and I did it once in a while myself." After picking up Rinette at the airport, he told her, "Let's go talk at Slide Mountain."

Peter was talking almost non-stop now to the investigators, the details of his lonely existence spilling out.

"We went up there and talked and, um, we were there probably an hour and I got out of the car and smoked a cigar," Peter said. "I think it's still out there in the road. I threw it out in the road when I was done. Um, and, uh, we talked and talked and talked and talked and, and, uh, the end of the conversation was, was, was pretty exciting for me 'cause she said that she would cut back on her travel and that she'd be home with me and I would not be alone like I have felt like I have been. Last year, she was gone almost three months of the year. I didn't sign up for this being gone. I want a wife who's home with me. That's, that's important to me and my life."

Up on the mountain "we started just chit-chat talk and just try to catch up from being gone for six weeks now and I said, 'Let's go down to the next level and look at the lights overlooking Reno to our left.'

"Well, we got down that way and I started to brake and I started to brake and I started to brake and it wasn't braking. It wasn't stopping. I couldn't figure out why it wasn't stopping and next thing I know I hit the guardrail and the next thing I'd wake up, I'm on the dirt and I don't see the car and I'm yelling for my wife. I don't know where she is. And that's all I remember what happened."

"OK," McLellan said, trying to digest this. "You're going to excuse me. I've been up for about twenty-four hours now."

McLellan asked Bergna to describe exactly where they were when they stopped to talk.

"We were just below the actual entrance to Slide Mountain Ski Area."

"You're talking about what's called East Bowl now?"

"Is that what it's called? Is that . . . OK, yeah, OK, East Bowl probably."

"There is a gate or some barrier?"

"There's two wide barriers and a metal fence if I recall correctly."

"And you were parked right at those?"

"Yeah, about two car lengths away. We went to the top, turned around, came down right there."

"You said you accelerated when you left?"

"Right, going down the hill."

"Do you know what speed you accelerated up to?"

"No. I've had a problem with my car," he said, beginning another long answer. The man did love to talk, and that was OK with the officers. There was no lawyer in the room. Bergna had just told the officers that shortly after discussing problems in his marriage, the source of those problems ended up dead in a car wreck that left Bergna with hardly a scratch.

"I had it looked at by Jones West Ford a couple weeks ago and sometimes after starting the car, after running it for a while going long distance, it'll hesitate and start off, and it seemed to do that a little bit as I was taking off," Bergna rambled on. "And so I know I gave it a little more juice to get it going and once it gets up a little bit, then it clears out, OK? Does that make sense, what I'm saying? We used to say that was a fuel filter problem or whatever. The engine light is still on now—at least it was this morning in the car, which tells me there's still something wrong with it. And so I accelerated to get over that little hesitation, and then, next thing I know, I'm getting close, I start to brake and I start to brake and I'm not braking. I'm not braking. It's not stopping. I'm panicking. It's not stopping. I'm braking. I'm braking. I'm braking. I'm pushing as hard as I can and nothing's happening."

"You said this [fuel problem] has occurred?"

"Right."

"At what speed did it normally clear out?"

"Within about fifteen, twenty miles per hour, maybe ten miles per hour, I don't know. I've never really watched it clear it. It just clears out after a couple seconds of acceleration, you know. I don't understand what it is. They say it's a computer problem or something, and they were supposed to have fixed it once before. It didn't get fixed."

"You got past the speed to work, it cleared out?"

"Or seemed like it, yes."

"Then you attempted to brake?"

"Right."

"You noticed that you're rolling up [to the guardrail]?"

"Rolling up to the guardrail to stop and overlook the valley."

"What happened during the braking? You said you were applying the brakes?"

"I was . . . I was . . . I was . . . I was almost out of my seat pressing down on that brake as hard as I could press it down to the floor." Bergna told them that he had told a friend after the accident that about a year-and-a-half earlier he had had a similar brake problem. "I was going in the driveway and I was trying to stop the car and I was pressing as hard as I could on the brake and it wasn't stopping," he recalled relating to this friend. "I was hitting the accelerator. I was not [hitting] the brake pedal."

"OK," said McLellan, "when you realized you were going towards the guardrail, what did you do? I mean, you're applying the brakes?"

"I think."

"Or you thought you were applying the brakes?"

"I don't know if I . . . I don't remember if I turned the . . . I don't remember if I turned the wheel or anything else. I was just trying to stop. That's all I was trying to do was stop. That's all I was trying to do. I had my window open 'cause I just got through smoking a cigar."

"Has it ever had a brake problem before?"

"No, not at all."

Beltron then interjected. "I just have one question," asked the detective, recalling that he had seen no skid marks or brake fluid at the scene. "You said you hit the brakes, but then your friend said you may have hit the accelerator. Do you remember hitting the brakes?"

"That's a good question," said Bergna. "I drive twenty thousand to forty thousand miles a year. Doesn't answer your question, but I drive all over the state of California, Nevada, never got a ticket, never got in an accident. I'd swear to you, I was hitting the brakes. I swear I was hitting the brakes."

"Well, that . . . that's . . ." said Beltron.

"But I don't know for a fact that . . ."

"You don't want to put things in your own head that confuse you. If you hit the brakes, you hit the brakes," said Beltron.

"I don't know if I was."

McLellan then resumed the questioning. "You picked your wife up at the airport?"

"I went down and picked her up, met her at the airport."

"You go up there quite often, you said?" McLellan asked, referring to the road on Slide Mountain where the accident occurred.

"You know, every couple months."

"To look out over the lights?"

"I . . . I . . . I . . . I grew up in the Bay Area," Bergna said. "My folks had a house up on top of the hill overlooking the valley, and I just always loved that, and that, just to me, is wonderful to look over the valley and see the lights and see the hills and so forth. I mean, once in a while, see a shooting star. I think it's one of the best places I know to go do that. It's not like a weekly occurrence. It might be every couple months we might go up there for an hour or two."

"Do you ski? I mean, would you go up there for skiing?"

"I do ski, but I've not skied probably for ten, twelve years."

"I'm just trying to figure out how familiar you are with the road and the turns and stuff in it," McLellan said.

"If I've been up there, in my eleven years up here at Tahoe, if I've gone up there five, six times, I'd be lucky."

The investigators were surprised.

Earlier, Peter called the area where he took his wife one of their favorite spots to sit and watch the lights. Then he said he had maybe been there five or six times in the last eleven years.

A favorite spot he rarely visited.

Peter was contradicting himself—and not for the first time. The story he was laying out was making no sense. The man is lonely for his wife, he drives up to the side of a mountain in the middle of night, they have a discussion about the state of their marriage, and then somehow— Peter doesn't remember how—the car goes off the cliff. He didn't know if he was braking or not braking, but he was pretty sure the truck had no history of brake problems.

People act in strange and sometimes inappropriate ways after a tragedy like this, and the investigators were going to give Peter the benefit of all the doubt they could.

They were also going to try to keep him talking.

Without a lawyer in the room.

Chapter 9

"Do you need anything to drink?" Detective Beltron asked.

"No, I got . . . They gave me some pills," Bergna said. "I don't know what it's going to do to me here but I think I'm fine at this point."

"That's what my next question was," Beltron said. The detective wanted to make sure that Peter was completely coherent during this interview; he didn't want a lawyer later claiming that it was the drugs—and not Peter—doing the talking. "I know your friends met me at the door and they said they gave you some medication. You're aware of what's going on?"

"Yeah, I'm very much aware, yeah."

"OK, you're aware of what you're saying?"

"Yeah, there's no problem. . . . If I have a problem, then I will tell you that I can't go any further."

"All right. Well, we're not here to do that to you."

"No. I understand. I understand."

McLellan then asked, "I understand from the trooper

that came to the hospital to see you that you had taken Vicodin, I believe?"

"No. It's a pain pill and it may be a Tylenol codeine. I got more at home. I could show you which one it is. I thought it was Vicodin. It may not have been a Vicodin. You know, my wife's the one that knows all the pills. I know it's a painkiller. My back's been bothering me when I work out a lot. You need a muscle relaxer, but that's the only thing I got that's powerful enough to give me some relief, so . . ."

His wife would know, he said. But his wife was dead.

Now, McLellan wanted to slow things down. This wasn't going to be just any accident probe—there were too many red flags—and he wanted to make what he was doing very clear to Bergna. Slowly, he asked Bergna, "One of the things that I have to do for when someone's been— I need to reconstruct that person's last twenty-four hours.

"So do you know," asked McLellan, "what time she left Italy? Is that where she was?"

"She was in Italy," said Bergna. "I don't know where in Italy she was. I mean, that would not be hard to find out. She just told me that she was going to fly from Italy to New York to Salt Lake City and the plane was to come in between nine-thirty and ten-thirty, so I called Delta and said, 'Hi, when's the next flight in from Salt Lake City?' It was ten-fifteen, ten-twenty, somewhere in that ballpark."

"So she was on Delta?"

"On Delta Airlines."

Beltron asked, "Do you know who she booked it with?"

"It was booked through Tauck Tours. You know Tauck is spelled funny, It's T-A-U-C-K, something like that. Tauck. Tauck Tours of Connecticut."

Chapter 10

"We are a family company, built on a timeless philosophy of integrity, innovation and respect"

—Tauck Tour mission statement

In the mid-1920s, a traveling salesman named Arthur Tauck traveled New England in a Studebaker peddling his invention, an aluminum coin tray used in banks. He soon found that it was the scenery and history of the region, not the sales calls, that captured his attention. He began bringing friends along on his treks, offering his own commentary on the sights. By the end of the decade, a tour agency was born, with Tauck himself leading the journeys at the wheel of a seven-passenger car.

Seventy years later, Tauck Tours had far outgrown that touring car. Now known by the more exciting name of Tauck World Discovery, the company has become a major player in the travel industry. Run by Arthur Tauck's grandchildren, the company offers tours by bus, rail and sailboat on seven continents, from Canada to Antarctica, with the promise of "enriching and inspiring travel experiences."

It was during a Tauck Tours trip through Australia in 1996 that Rinette got the idea. She asked her tour guide what it would take to get a job with Tauck. What she heard thrilled her. What had been a hobby was now going to be her life. After she returned from Australia, she decided to give up her career as a pharmacist and called Tauck Tours for an employment application.

On January 14, 1997, Rinette was interviewed by phone by a Tauck representative and took Tauck's personality test, which seeks people who are both gregarious and intelligent. The bubbly, PhD-holding Rinette passed with flying colors. She was referred to Tauck's Kendra St. John, who was in charge of hiring and training tour directors.

On May 18, 1997, St. John spoke with Rinette by phone from St. John's office in Connecticut. "I thought she was ideal for the job," St. John would recall. "She was extremely intelligent, but also very caring—smart enough to learn everything she needed to know about these places where she would be sent to take guests on tour, and yet very warm and caring and friendly to make them feel comfortable and have a good time." A good enough time that they would come back again, providing the vital repeat business. Rinette spoke of her love of Europe, particularly Italy, where she had relatives in the Lake Como area near the Swiss border. Rinette spoke fluent Italian and knew enough French to carry on a conversation. "Even though I was very impressed with her, we had a policy not to hire people on the phone, but always want to think overnight and let them have a chance to think about it overnight at least," said St. John. "I called her the next day and offered her the job."

Two months later, Rinette Riella-Bergna, well-paid pharmacist, had become a trainee tour guide, tagging along with a guide and his group on a tour to Williamsburg, Virginia, and Washington, DC, from July 27 to August 3, 1997, watching the guide in action, taking notes and boning up on the local color and history. The day after that tour ended, she was in the classroom in Seattle for four days. It was there that she met St. John face-to-face. "I liked her very much," St. John later recalled. "[We] bonded, you know. I felt very comfortable talking with her. I respected her intelligence and her honesty and her willingness to try something new after many years of doing the same thing. She was very excited about this new career." After Seattle, it was off to the East Coast again for another training tour of Williamsburg from August 17 to August 24. She was given a couple of weeks off to study her notes and get organized, then she led her first tours—six one-week tours, all back-to-back, in Williamsburg, starting September 12, 1997. She would drop one group off at the airport and pick up another, a common practice for peak season, which runs May through October, when a guide could work for five months with only three or four days off.

Life on the move, away from pills and prescriptions, was everything that Rinette dreamed it would be. She had taken a monster pay cut—earning about half her $100,000 salary—and the hours were punishing and the work non-stop, but she loved it, so much so that almost immediately she began lobbying Tauck for a more ambitious assignment than week-long treks through Williamsburg. She wanted Europe.

Normally, this is a tall order. Tauck traditionally wanted guides to learn their business on the shorter US tours, which are less expensive and extensive. But as it happened, the demand for tours to Europe, particularly Italy, heading into the spring and summer of 1998, was growing. The fact that Rinette had done well in the United States—Tauck received glowing letters from customers—and the fact that she spoke Italian and had family in the area, were enough to convince Tauck to send a rookie overseas. "We really needed her, and it was just a perfect natural fit," said St. John. Spring is the second-busiest time for European tours, after fall—it's too hot in the summer for many travelers' tastes—so Rinette was put on the fast track.

In March 1998, Rinette brought Peter to Las Vegas for a conference for tour directors. It was here that he and St. John met and found they had gone to the same college and both knew the same soccer coach. St. John had a good impression of Peter. "He said when I was talking with him that it seemed like a great job, and if he wasn't so involved with his antique business it would be something he'd be interested in," she recalled.

A month after the conference, Rinette headed for Europe. The itinerary called for the trip to begin with a training tour to Italy from April 22, 1998, to May 4, 1998. She then planned to stay with relatives in Lake Como before leaving for a second training tour from May 8 to 17. After five more days off, which she again planned to spend with the Lake Como relatives, she would lead her first tour, taking a group through Italy for ten days from May 22 to May 31. She would then return to the United States for a break. In all, she would be on the road for more than a month, from late April to the end of May. And this time, unlike the quick trip to Vegas for the tour director conference, Peter wasn't going to be with her.

Such long stretches away from home and loved ones are common in the tour business. St. John would explain to investigators that it cost Tauck Tours about $5,000 to send Rinette on the two training tours to Italy alone—that included industry-discounted meals, rooms and flights—and the company wanted to make sure she was committed for the long haul. Ten to twelve straight weeks on the road is a normal assignment for an international tour guide. And while spouses and significant others are welcome to join tour guides wherever they are on their days off, they have to pay for it. This was made very clear to Rinette, and she accepted it. She told Tauck that aside from a few dates she couldn't work because of a pharmacy conference or an antiques-hunting road trip with her husband, she was fully prepared to make that time commitment.

Peter, however, was another story. "I think I saw some disappointment in Peter," said his friend, Gary Espinosa, "but I think there's an understanding where she was going to be gone maybe weeks to days, but maybe months of the year. I think there was some discussion, but I didn't think it was serious. I think it was something they were going to have to settle." His friend Mark Sampson said, "When Rinette wanted to become a tour agent, spending a number of days and weeks [away], I think Peter missed her. I think he felt lonely without her and would have preferred if she had a different type of job that allowed her to stay home more." Peter's employee Adelaide Gramanz said that Rinette's month away in Europe took him by surprise. "It was very short notice," she would recall. "I think she had thought she was going to be doing some East Coast tours maybe for one or two weeks at a time. When she got to Europe, that was a huge kind of bonus. It really came up out of the blue." She said that Peter hadn't thought it all through. "I mean, I think he hadn't really mentally prepared himself for her being gone for such a long period," said Gramanz.

But away Rinette went, on the two training tours and then on the ten-day tour she led herself. And this wasn't going to be the end of it. St. John said that after the Italy tour, Rinette was set to head out in early July to Williamsburg for three weeks, followed by another tour of the

Eastern US in late August. Although not on the agenda, "She was excited about going back to Italy," St. John said. She was so excited that, according to her cousin in Italy, Gianna Riella, Rinette had looked into buying a condominium near her cousin's Lake Como home. While staying with Gianna between tours, Rinette spoke to a real estate agent about buying a unit in a condominium complex that was under construction for about $150,000. According to the cousin, Rinette was holding off on a decision until September to see what the condo units actually looked like when completed.

The longer Rinette was gone, the more Peter would complain about how much he missed her. "He is a very social person," said Gramanz. "He didn't like being alone. He really tried to fill up the time." He would go to sporting events at the high school at night, or spend time with friends. He would take trips for business, among them the journey to Portland, Oregon, in his truck that he told investigators about. But most nights, he would complain, were spent alone, in front of the television set, and he only rarely communicated with Rinette because the long-distance charges were so steep.

One such call came around May 26, 1998, with less than a week left before Rinette's return. Rinette had sent Peter a telefax from the Hotel Excelsior in Florence, Italy. The note betrayed no hint of any tension between Rinette and Peter, as she discussed the trip and their friend, soccer coach Mark Steven Sampson.

> *Dear Peterski,*
> *Hope you had a great time in Oregon. I've been watching Steve on TV here. They've been giving a lot of coverage to Preki. They are predicting a possible train and truck strike in France during World Cup. I'll try and call you later today. If I can't*

reach you today, I will call tomorrow. I am going to dinner about 7:30, 10:30 your time. . . . See you Sunday.

       Love
       Nette.

Five days after sending that telefax, Peter Bergna would pick up his wife from the airport and drive her up the side of the mountain.

Chapter 11

"What time did you get up yesterday?"

"Yesterday morning," Peter told Trooper McLellan, "I got up, um, about seven, six o'clock, seven o'clock, somewhere in that neighborhood, which is normal for me."

"Do you normally eat breakfast?" asked the trooper.

"No. I'm trying to think if I ate breakfast. OK, yeah, I went down to the Walkers'. The Walkers have eight kids, and those have become my kids because, uh, we don't have children."

The Walkers lived around the corner from the Bergnas. Like Rinette, they were Catholic. They attended the same church in Incline Village. Unlike Rinette, Sherry Walker was a mother, eight times over.

Peter arrived at the Walker home around 8:30 a.m. "I stayed and watched cartoons with the kids, and they gave me a Costco muffin"—Costco is a discount warehouse store. "I forget if it was blueberry or poppy seed or something like that."

Peter's recollections of the morning were a little fuzzy—so many kids and so many activities—but the morning revolved around breakfast, cartoons and God. The Walker clan went to Mass in shifts, some at 9 a.m., the others for the 11 a.m. service, and Peter watched various Walker children while the others were at church. After the 11 a.m. Mass, Peter joined the entire Walker family for lunch at Joe's Café, in an Incline Village casino. Afterwards, some of the Walker children went to Peter's house. "The three little ones wanted to come up and watch movies at my house 'cause we have all these Disney movies and stuff," he told the investigators. "We watched a Disney movie. I forget which one it was."

At about 4 p.m. on Sunday, May 31, 1998, Peter drove the Walker children home, then joined the Walker parents in attending the Incline High School Boosters' Appreciation Night event at a hotel.

"A group of people had been working on booster staff to raise money for the athletic program for the school all year long," Bergna said, "and they put on a dinner for us and they served steak and chicken and wine and Cokes and so forth, and dips and so forth and so on," he said. He said he then went back to the Walkers' house and watched a televised soccer match between the US national team and Scotland.

At 9 p.m., he left for Reno to pick up his wife at the airport, stopping along the way to fuel up his truck.

"I was planning to go to Vegas on Wednesday and I filled up two extra gas cans to take me to Vegas," he said.

That was the first statement that directly related to evidence found at the scene: the two plastic gas cans amid the wreckage on the cliff. Beltron, who had been involved in picking up the cans, had wondered from the beginning why the truck was carrying extra gas. The gas cans, combined with the lack of skid marks—or any other evidence of an accident—struck Beltron as suspicious. The cans were torn apart in the crash, but the truck had not blown up; in fact, it's rare for a vehicle to explode in a crash, even a violent one, and even if there are gas cans aboard. That's the stuff of movies.

Beltron then picked up the questioning.

"When you went to Reno to get fuel, where did you get fuel at? Do you remember?"

"I don't normally go there. Went to, I think AM/PM, South Virginia, I think it was. Right across from Taco Bell. Kitty-corner to Taco Bell. I'm on the road, I know these places pretty well."

Bergna was telling the truth. A gas station security video would show him filling up.

"And did you pay for it with cash?" asked Beltron.

"I paid cash for it, yeah."

"OK, how much fuel did you buy?"

"I bought forty dollars even. Total. My main tank was on empty and I planned it that way to be down there so I could fill the tank," he said, explaining he was headed to Las Vegas "in a day or two" and that he also needed extra gas in the cans for the lawn mower.

McLellan interjected, "That metal or plastic?" He knew the answer. He wanted to see what Peter would say.

"They were plastic."

The trooper continued, "You have one tank on your truck and then you filled up those other two?"

"That is correct, yeah," said Bergna. "I . . . just . . . going to Vegas from here, I've done it a couple times—real scary, gas prices could be high and so forth, and I try to prepare for things before they happen so they don't happen. You know, if they happen, I'm prepared for it."

The investigators wondered if Peter, in buying the extra gas, hadn't been preparing for something besides a long trip to Vegas. Like his claim that the brakes didn't work, Peter's explanation for the gas cans seemed implausible—and inconsistent. At times he said he needed the extra gas to save a couple dollars from higher-priced stations in the remote desert towns south of Reno. At other times, he said he needed the gas for the lawn mower.

Beltron asked, "Your wife has been gone for six weeks?"

"Six weeks."

"What was life like before that for you two?"

"Well, it was very good," said Bergna. "I was encouraging her to take this tour job" and leave the pharmacy business, he said. "She really, really is excited about traveling. It's been a fetish of hers since, she's told me, through high school about traveling and so forth."

The investigators paused to savor the word "fetish."

Peter acknowledged that he and his wife would occasionally argue "like most couples" about small aggravations such as finances and taking out the trash. "Other than that, I think we had a pretty good life," he said, and he spoke of their travels together or with his parents to Monterey or to Portland to watch the US soccer team play. Bergna said he was a big soccer fan, which explained his vanity license plate: FIFA is the Federation Internationale de Football Assocation, the governing body for international soccer. "We have a lot of fun, a lot of fun," he said. "That's just the hardest thing for me, 'cause I just kept telling her I do not want to be alone. I did not want to be alone."

"When you were up there on the side of the road," McLellan asked, "what was the conversation like?"

"It was peaceful," said Bergna, and then he seemed to reverse course. "It got a little loud a couple times, but we both realized we wanted to work some things out to where she knew I was frustrated with her schedule of being gone six weeks at a time, and that was very tough on me being home."

Without being asked, he said that he didn't "fool around" and that he went out dancing one night—"the first time in fifteen years, God almighty. But other than that, I don't go out. I don't go hit the bars. I'm not out looking for women. I stay home. And that gets someone like myself lonely, and I did not like to do that, and so I expressed that opinion to her that I was very unhappy in that respect and I wanted to have—hope she would change. We talked about compromise. . . . My love is antiques. I know if she took away my antiques, I'd be devastated. . . . But [if] she said, you know, 'Can you curtail them for a little bit and do something else with me?' I would say, 'Yeah, I could curtail them.' Could I stop them? No, I wouldn't want to stop them. I wouldn't want her to stop her travel. That's just her love and it's her love. She loves it. The woman got excited going to the airport. Just going to the airport, she got excited."

Beltron asked, "Now did either of you get out of the vehicle up there?"

"I did 'cause I was smoking a cigar."

"Where did you leave the vehicle at?"

"The side of the road."

"I mean, what part of the area? Did you just have it parked and way away or . . ."

"We left, I drove to the white barriers and came back down and turned around, maybe a hundred yards or so from the top . . . and then I parked." He continued, "She doesn't like me to smoke in the house or the car, so I was polite enough to go outside and smoke my cigar, and did that, and we were talking. I was, you know, just kind of walking around a little bit outside and smoking my cigar."

"What kind of shoes were you wearing?" Beltron asked. He had found some shoe prints in the dirt.

"My white tennis shoes."

Beltron asked if Bergna still had the shoes. He told him he'd had them on when he got to the hospital along with the rest of his clothing. "When I got in the accident I had on a pair of white shoes, a pair of Levi's, a yellow shirt, my Incline High School athletic sweatshirt and then a green jacket," he said. "Oh, I had a pair of gloves too 'cause it got cold. I put my gloves on." He said when he left the hospital, all he had were the pants.

Without telling Peter, Beltron considered the clothing as critical evidence. Investigators would get nearly everything Peter was wearing that night and send it to the crime lab. The clothing, Beltron felt, could help re-create what happened on the mountain and, most important, answer the question of when Peter left the truck. Since the driver's-side airbag deployed during the crash, the cab of the truck would have been filled with a powdery substance used to lubricate the airbag. Beltron knew from investigating other accidents that this substance was usually a fine cornstarch. The detective wanted to examine Peter's clothing to see if it was covered in this organic lubricant.

If it was, that meant he was in the cab at the time the airbag deployed, either when the truck hit the guardrail or when it hit the ground. This would support the contention that the crash was a tragic accident.

But if there was no cornstarch on the clothing, this would suggest Peter was *not* in the truck when it went over the side.

And that, Beltron knew, would be evidence of a possible homicide.

"Now," Beltron asked, "during your heated exchanges, was there any physical contact?"

"No, none whatsoever. No."

"Now, you said that you don't go to bars and pick up on people. Was there ever a problem with that with your wife?"

"With her doing it?"

"Right."

"Oh, no."

"No? OK."

"Not even close. We're two pretty committed people. What we believe in our relationship, we think it's right and we stick to it. We don't go out and fool around. Never, ever. I would never do it to her and she would never do it to me, and I believe that in all sincerity."

McLellan asked, "Do you and your wife normally wear your seatbelts? I'm pretty sure you weren't wearing yours."

"She does religiously," he said, but noted that he doesn't have the same commitment.

"Did your wife have hers on tonight?" asked McLellan, knowing that she had.

"I, yeah, I believe she did. Yes. Uh-huh. I believe she did. And I know I had the airbag turned off for her because she's a small person and I've been told recently in the last two months that [with] a small person I should turn off the airbag on that side, so I had the airbag off. I don't know if that would have made a difference, if she would be alive now if I had the thing on or not. I have no idea, but I was told to turn it off for a small person, so I did."

The officers got another surprise: They knew that the passenger-side airbag had not gone off. Now they knew why.

"How tall?" asked McLellan.

"Four-foot-nine. She's not even five feet. Uh, one hundred twenty pounds or something like that."

Short, a little overweight—and making him lonely. Investigators wondered what Peter really felt about his wife.

Beltron announced he was flipping over the tape, then when side B came on he announced the time was 11:29 a.m. "Mr. Bergna, did anybody ask you any questions while the tape was turned?"

"No."

And as questioning resumed, Peter would drop a surprise.

Chapter 12

"OK, have you ever been up in that area when people are hang-gliding?"

Beltron knew that the crash site was also a popular hang-gliding launch pad. He also knew that Peter had already given inconsistent statements about how many times he and Rinette had been there. At one point, Peter called it their favorite romantic spot where they could see the lights of Reno. At another point, he said he had only been there five or six times in the last decade.

Maybe, Beltron thought, he could get a clarification— or perhaps even a third account.

He didn't expect what Peter would say next.

Peter had been to the site the day before the crash.

He said he had gone there with his friend Allan Walker's brother, Doug, and two of the Walker children whom Peter so adored. It was on Saturday, May 30, 1998.

"I took them out there and we talked about hang gliders

for about ten minutes or so and then drove back down the hill and came home," Peter said.

"OK," replied Beltron, "did you get out and walk around then?"

"I think I walked," Peter said. "The kids wanted to go over to the bench, so I went over [to] the bench with the kids too, so they wouldn't, you know, jump it or something and get dangerous. So I went with the kids and we walked, I don't know, over to the fence and back over to the hang gliders and back over to the car, I think. We didn't do too much really. They got a little scared. It was too steep for them."

The investigators thought it was an incredible admission: Not only had Peter been to the scene the day before the crash, but he got a good enough look, by daylight, to know how steep and scary it was.

Beltron asked about Walker's brother and got a phone number, then abruptly changed the subject, returning to Peter's recollections of the crash. It's an old police interrogation trick—don't stay on any one subject too long so that the person gets too comfortable.

"I didn't quite catch it," Beltron said, "now did you say you lost steering or was there a problem with your steering?"

Here, Bergna, who could remember what store had sold the muffin he ate the previous morning, stumbled over his words, his memory as fuzzy about the steering as it was about the brakes. "No problem with my steering," he said. "I, I, I think I said it, it, I don't remember if I, if I was trying to counteract the steering or, or correct the steering to make a, a turn. All I remember was just trying to brake and being frustrated that I couldn't brake."

The investigators changed the subject again, to the amount of luggage Rinette had, to what she was wearing.

They then asked him about the paperback books strewn down the hillside.

"Oh, I brought them," said Peter. "I go out to garage sales and flea markets every weekend and buy stuff, you know, that's just kind of been a hobby for twenty years. . . . They were probably good books. Probably shit now, but . . ."

"There were a lot," observed McLellan, who, like the other investigators, marveled at the fact that Peter showed concern about the loss of his paperbacks. Yet not once did he ask anything about Rinette or the circumstances of her death. Instead, his mind was on cheap books and other finds, and while the operation of his truck's brakes and steering at the moment of the crash created some confusion in Peter's mind, he knew all about those books.

"There was, um, thirty of them," he said. "Half a dollar apiece. I bought them in the morning. That's a good point, too. I didn't talk about my garage sale. Forgot all about that one."

Beltron asked, "Did your wife call you while she was gone?"

"Yes, she did," said Peter. "And I'll be happy to show you these several-hundred-dollar bills. Shit. I love my wife dearly, I really do, but we talked from Italy and Italy's not cheap. We're talking for an hour and a half."

Peter related that he once went to a Las Vegas seminar on relationships. "The big thing is, how do you communicate with someone that's far away? Do you write them a letter every day? Do you e-mail them? Do you send them cards and flowers and, you know, phone calls and stuff? But we went the phone call route, and, I wouldn't have done that again."

"How many times do you think she called you in six weeks?"

"She probably called me—'cause I could never get

ahold of her 'cause her schedule's so screwy—once a week maybe. And two times we talked for over an hour and a half." He said they would ask each other how things were going—"no big deal"—but the calls were "very lengthy."

"How long has she been talking about changing jobs?"

"We went on a Tauck Tour with my parents to Australia. I'm not good with dates or time. I mean, it's got to be two years ago. We went to Australia with my mom and dad and she got back thinking. . . . She came back saying, 'I can do this.' And I said, 'You should do that. I think you should do that.' I'm willing to encourage my wife to be the best she can be. I'm just, I'm very positive that way. Not only with her, but kids in the community. You talk to anybody at the high school who knows me and I'm [a] very— you know—giving, encouraging, positive, motivated-type person."

Why, wondered the investigators, did Peter want them to check his references?

"I said [to Rinette], 'Whatever you want to do, then go do it,'" Peter rambled on. "I said, 'You love to travel. I know you love to travel'—and travel is not my thing. I do travel and I have been overseas and such, but her real passion in life— She loves it. I read a book; she wanted to read about traveling so she could travel more."

McLellan asked, "Did your wife just do the Italy trips?"

"No, she was so thrilled, she was absolutely thrilled to get this tour. When she came out of tour guide school, they told her that you don't normally get a job for the first three to five years because there's such a backlog of tour guides and so forth and so on, and you're not experienced and so forth. But she traveled the world so much, she graduated first in her class, which never surprised me 'cause the woman is—I don't know—she's in the genius category. . . . If I could have anybody by my side if I were dying, I want my wife at my side. That woman knew more about medicine and how to take care of [people]. The woman's unbelievable."

If Bergna recognized the perverse irony of what he had just said, he didn't remark about it. Rather, he kept talking, going on about her tour director training.

They discussed the truck again, its good maintenance history, its engine power, before Beltron got back to what Peter and Rinette were doing up on the mountain.

"Did you and your wife ever argue outside the truck up there?"

"Well, I was outside. I mean, is that what you're saying? I was out and she was in?"

"No, were both of you ever outside the vehicle on the side of the road?"

"You asked me that before, and I don't recall her being out there with me."

Up until this point, Sergeant Butko had said nothing. He'd listened while Beltron and McLellan did the questioning.

No more.

"OK," Butko said, "let me ask you a question."

"Sure," said Peter.

"Were you aware that there is a caretaker that stays at that building?"

Butko didn't say where "that building" was located, but the implication would be clear—near the turnout where Peter and Rinette were discussing their marriage, in the quiet of the night.

"No," said Peter.

"Were you guys arguing in such a manner where somebody could hear you?" asked Butko.

"I mean, I'm a loud per— I have a loud voice, you know," said Peter, rattled.

"But that isn't what I asked."

"Oh."

"What were you arguing about and was it loud enough where somebody could have overheard it?"

"Somebody could have heard me," Peter said. I guess the answer would prob— might be yes. With the mountains up there, it could echo across and so forth, yeah."

"All right. Then what were you arguing about?" asked Butko.

"Uh, about, about staying home. About, about, uh, staying home with me and not leaving and about the fact that I've wanted children all my life and so forth and she does not."

"Did she discuss, uh, divorcing you?"

"That . . . That was . . . That was brought up as a possibility."

Peter had downplayed the seriousness of the talk on the mountain, saying only that they'd discussed her traveling and his loneliness, and that they had come to an amicable agreement that she would travel less and he wouldn't be so lonely. Then they would look at the lights.

This was the first time he mentioned divorce. The possibility that the caretaker had heard this seemed to force the admission.

"Did she ever threaten . . . uh . . . want to take your antiques from you?" Butko asked.

"You know, I think I told her I didn't want her to take my antiques from her . . . or . . . I didn't want her to take my antiques from me."

"I'm sorry for interjecting, Jim." And Butko was quiet again for the rest of the interview, but he had done what he meant to do.

There was no caretaker.

Butko made it up. A phantom witness to provoke a genuine answer.

From this point on, the caretaker seemed to weigh on Bergna, and he would return to it near the end of the questioning.

They later interrupted the interview long enough to take pictures of Bergna's head, foot and hands. By now it was two minutes after noon.

Chapter 13

"Do you have any death benefits for your wife, life insurance . . . ?"

It's a standard question in a death investigation, and Beltron fully expected the answer he got.

"We do, yes."

Couples of the financial standing of the Bergnas are usually well insured, and the fact that Rinette had $250,000 in life insurance was standard, perhaps even a little low. What *was* unexpected was what Peter said next.

Rinette stood to inherit property from her family. It was farmland in the Central Valley where she grew up.

"And what would you think that would be worth?" Beltron asked.

"You know, they go round and round anywhere from seven hundred thousand, six—six—I'd say six to eight hundred thousand, somewhere in that ballpark there."

The insurance plus the inheritance made the ballpark worth a cool million.

If the crash was determined to be an accident, it was

all but certain Peter would get the quarter-million-dollar insurance payout. The question was whether he would also qualify for Rinette's inheritance. Beltron asked Peter about it briefly, and Peter suggested that he might not. "It was a family deal," he said. "Spouses don't get involved, only the blood."

Actually, investigation would later find this wasn't entirely true. Nor, it turned out, was Peter's description of the insurance.

The insurance policy had gone into effect on August 13, 1997—nine months before the accident. Under the terms, Rinette and Bergna each had not only the $250,000 in term life insurance, but an additional $200,000 each that Peter didn't mention in the interview. This money covered accidental death—as in a truck crash. The couple's insurance broker would later insist that Bergna didn't want this much insurance—that the $250,000 was Rinette's idea, while Bergna wanted much less. The broker said it was he who pushed the relatively low-cost accidental death coverage. But the end result was that with Rinette dying an accidental death, Bergna stood to receive a check from the Safeco Insurance Company of Redmond, Washington, for a total of $450,000.

As for the inheritance, that was a more complicated matter. When Rinette's mother died in 1994, she and her two full brothers, Richard and Jack, drew up a partnership agreement by which each sibling would get a one-third share of the family farm, estimated to be valued at about $664,000. Richard still lived on the property and worked the farm, but each sibling was entitled to a share of the property worth about $220,000. As drafted by a lawyer, the agreement said that if one of the siblings died, that one-third share of the farm would go to the sibling's husband or wife.

But there was a catch.

The agreement said that the spouse had to sell his or her $220,000 to the other surviving siblings. The siblings had two years to come up with the money. That way, the farm stayed in the family. This is apparently what Peter meant when he said that spouses don't get involved.

This agreement was designed by Rinette and her brothers. "The three spouses had to sign, but they were not really involved," said Richard. "When we talked about business, it was just the three of us. We didn't do it with all the spouses."

As investigators would later find, this did not sit well with Peter. While the wives of the two Riella brothers accepted the deal, Peter didn't want to sign. He didn't like the economics of it. When Rinette's mother died, Peter had thought Rinette—and thus he, too—was $220,000 richer.

As long as the Riellas kept the land, all they would get would be the income from renting it out to other farmers— around $100 to $150 a month per acre. To Bergna, this was a lousy return and he thought the land should just be sold and the money invested in something better, like antiques. But Richard and his brother had no intention of selling a farm that had been in their family for generations. Richard said, "I had to make a few calls to my sister: 'Hey, you have to make him sign. Everybody's signed.' We had to get it. He finally signed begrudgedly."

And, now, he stood to expect about $220,000 within the next two years when Rinette's brothers bought him out. That, plus the insurance, made Rinette's death worth about $660,000, a little less than the million that investigators first thought Peter would get—but still a lot of money.

But there was one other issue that would be of great interest to investigators. As they waded through the complicated land-inheritance deal, they found something startling. Had Peter and Rinette divorced, he was entitled to nothing. Rinette would keep her share of the farm.

There was only one way Peter Bergna could get that $220,000 share.

Rinette had to die.

Chapter 14

The interview continued, and so did the contradictions.

Detective Beltron asked Peter if he had ever gone to the site of the crash before, besides that Saturday with Allan Walker's brother and the Walker children.

"No. Never," said Peter. "Never have."

Earlier he had said he had been there as many as six times.

Beltron asked: "Have you ever been there before with your wife?"

"Never have. Never have."

Earlier he had said the site was "one of our favorite spots."

"So it was just a verbal argument, that's it?" Beltron asked.

Peter waffled. He said "it was never a screaming match, never a yelling match." But there was that possibility of a caretaker up there. He acknowledged, "I might get a little loud." Peter talked about his and Rinette's bad ways with finances—how he had to take over the bills.

They discussed the truck's maintenance history, and Peter gave a long, rambling answer.

"How you feeling?" Beltron asked. "I want to make sure you're all right."

"I— I'm— I'm— I'm getting tired," Bergna admitted for the first time. "I'm— I'm— I'm— I'm conscious and— and— and— and I know what I'm saying and so forth."

"Well, I just want to make sure you're OK."

"Yeah."

"That's important to me."

"I'm— I'm the lucky one here at this point. I know I'm lucky. I know I'm lucky."

It was the first time Peter expressed concern about Rinette.

"Did you ever get down to the vehicle where it ended up?" Beltron asked.

"No. I— I— I— I was sliding down, grabbed onto rocks and whatever, I guess it's sagebrush down the hill and so forth, and I got to the point where I stopped. I was afraid to go any further not knowing I couldn't— My ankle hurt, my head hurt, I didn't know about my back. I— There was some pain in my back, I didn't want to turn over and— and start going down the hill. I turned around to kind of just glance. I could not see a thing. I started yelling and yelling and yelling and I would yell, and the 911 call. I yelled my wife's name several times, just to see if I could hear her, just so I could tell the lady on the 911 that she was OK, or something was going on and, and to help her. I mean, I knew I was hurt, but I wasn't the one in that car that went down five hundred, six hundred— I don't know how many feet it went down there. I mean, I knew she had more problems than I did and I was trying to get help, not for me, but for her. I knew I was going to be fine. I mean, I had an ankle problem here and a head problem here, but I knew she went down, and that was not good."

"Was your wife conscious when you were headed towards the guardrail?" Beltron asked.

"Oh, oh, yes. Oh, yeah, yeah."

"Was she screaming?"

"You know, I've stayed up for hours thinking about that, and I don't remember her screaming a bit. I don't remember her screaming."

"She didn't try to open up the door and leave the vehicle?"

"No."

"Did you open your door to leave the vehicle?"

"Had my window open, I remember that. I don't know if I did. I don't even know if my airbag deployed. I have no idea if it deployed or not. I don't recall it deploying. I just remember trying just to diligently hit the brake and hit that brake and it wasn't stopping."

"There's no [problem] with your steering?" Beltron asked.

"It's a good truck. I don't understand," Peter said.

Beltron said it appeared from the crash site that the truck went straight into the guardrail, rather than at an angle, suggesting that Peter would have had to have made a very sharp right turn.

"Right, right," said Peter.

Beltron asked Peter why he didn't just steer away from the guardrail. It was a wide, gentle curve. He couldn't have been going too fast—it was only a few hundred feet from where he started driving. The roadway was sloped, making it even easier to negotiate the turn.

Peter had no answer. "Only thing is that I— I— I think I focused on trying to stop the vehicle and that was it, then I started to panic."

"Huh."

"I panic when I go out of control, and I lost complete control at that point. In my mind I was losing control and I could— I couldn't stop it and I lost control, so now I'm panicking trying to get something to stop. I'm not thinking about turning, which I probably should be doing."

"I mean, I was out there," the investigator said, laying out some of the evidence for Peter for the first time. "There's no scuff, no skid, no gouge, no nothing—like a beeline. I don't understand if you know you're headed for the edge, either put it in a different gear—reverse, park, u-brake—or bail out. It looks like you bailed out, but it doesn't look like your wife bailed out, and that's why I asked if she was conscious."

"She was conscious."

"But you don't remember her screaming?"

"I don't remember. I don't remember her saying a word. I just, I just remember I was trying to brake and panicking because I couldn't get it to do what I know, after hundreds of thousands of miles, this thing should stop. If I'm hitting the right button, it should be stopping and it wasn't stopping."

"Where do you carry your cell phone at?"

"Uh, there's a, there's an apparatus in the front."

"So it's in, in the car-type holder?"

"Right, right. I pull it out once in a while when I go to soccer matches," he said, adding that this time it was in his pocket in case Rinette called him at the airport.

By now, the interview began skipping from subject to subject. Beltron returned to the state of the Bergna marriage, and Peter again spoke about how he didn't want to be alone. He also revealed that this was his second marriage. His first had ended some twenty years earlier after counseling couldn't resolve their differences. He said that he and Rinette had not gone to counseling.

The interview skipped back to the discussion on the

mountain, with Peter offering his musings on the best way to make a marriage work: "You're constantly trying to compromise on one another's ideas," he said.

"She never got physical with you?" asked Beltron.

"No."

"OK," Beltron said.

"I wish she had once in a while," Peter said. "It'd be kind of fun, but, no."

Neither had been drinking, said Peter, though he did note he had a 200-bottle wine cellar and that the couple would occasionally imbibe.

"We enjoy nice wine, but that's about where it ends," he said.

"Did she kiss you when she got off the plane?" asked Beltron.

"You bet. I gave her a hug, gave her a hug and a half."

"And she wasn't cold to you?"

"Oh, God, no," and on went Peter on another long answer about how the couple worked out their problems. "I don't want to be a dictator in a relationship and I don't want her to be the dictator to me," he said.

"Is there a reason that you can't have children?" asked Beltron. "Was it physical? Was it you?"

"Um, it wasn't me. I mean, I don't know if I could have 'em to tell you honestly, OK. I assumed I could. I was adopted to begin with, so whether I adopted or not, I didn't really care. She at some point, decided she did not want kids, and she told me one time that she couldn't have kids and one time she just did not want to have kids and listening to Dr. Laura on talk radio."

"Well, yeah, Dr. Laura, I listen to her."

"I listen to her all the time. I agree with her philosophy and that is, if the two of you don't want children, you should not have children."

"Right."

"And that was a real kind of bone of contention for me. I really wanted children, and I mean, if I agree with her from day one, right, and I agree with that not to have children, but the Walker children, who have eight in their family . . ."

Beltron said, "I have to stop the tape."

"OK."

"OK, we're turning the tape. It's twelve-thirty. . . . OK, transcriber, it's still twelve-thirty. Tape's been turned over. Mr. Bergna, did anybody ask you any questions while the tape was being turned?"

"No."

One of the officers asked, "Your first marriage—how long were you with your first wife?"

"I think it was about a year, a year and a half at the most."

"OK. You've never been arrested for any type of spousal battery?"

"Oh, God, no, no. My father was a DA for twenty-five years."

"Really?"

This was the first the investigators had known that Peter Bergna came from a law-enforcement family.

"Yes," said Peter. "Santa Clara County. We had a pretty strict household."

"Yes."

"My dad was very, very strict with all of us kids all the time, and I think now we're all pretty good kids because of it. We need to have more of those kind of parents out there."

A short time later, Peter revealed his knowledge of police matters when he recounted his ordeal on the mountain.

He knew that his 911 call would be recorded.

"When I, when I finally figured out where I was, it was on the sand, I was sliding down the hill, I'm trying to the best I could, looked up and see if I could see the truck, see a fire, see something, yelling for her," he said. "And I think you can check 911 tapes, I yelled, kind of yelled a lot. I was yelling her name constantly. Just try and see if I could hear her voice."

The interview was now nearly over. There were a couple more questions about Rinette's inheritance.

Beltron looked at McLellan and Butko.

"Any further questions?" asked Beltron.

McLellan said, "No."

But then Bergna had a question.

"Just out of curiosity," he asked, "where is, where is that care–caretaker's house? Is it behind the, the, the cement wall there, whatever?"

Butko stumbled, then recovered. "Um, uh, off to the left," he said.

"Off to the left?"

"Uh-huh."

"So whoever got there . . . I remember a skier there also," said Peter.

There was no skier—it wasn't clear what Peter was talking about—but Beltron seized on it. "And he, and he's being interviewed now, so we— we're waiting to be called from them."

First a phantom caretaker, now a phantom skier.

The officers saw Bergna's continued worry about the caretaker as an opportunity to push the interview further.

"Do you owe anybody any money, other than normal bills?" asked Beltron.

"Normal bills . . . No. No, let me just double-check here and see. Um, no, I just paid my house off and I'm very happy with that."

"Does anybody owe you money?"

"My wife does. She did."

His wife owed him money?

"Uh, she kind of went on a little spending spree and we got [down] about eighteen thousand dollars. We have, we have kind of separate accounts because she has her pharmacy business over here and her travel business over here, besides being in the tour guide business."

Beltron asked how Rinette would pay back $18,000 to Peter.

"Oh, by, by working. I mean, she went through this slow time where the consulting business kind of dropped for a while and so forth. She was doing some, uh, dispensing of medication and then, then the tour company came on with their program."

"Uh-huh."

"And once that happened, I knew, you know, it'd be a matter of months and I'll be paid back and so I wasn't too worried about it. So, oh, my nephew owes me some money, little sucker. Um, I lent him three thousand dollars for a car, yeah. He pays it back once in a while. Not doing too badly."

"Now, you say that you were arguing—substantially different than just, just arguing. It wasn't just loud. There was name-calling and things like that, from the caretaker?" asked Beltron, invoking the fake witness.

"He said we were— I was calling her names and so forth?" asked Peter.

"Just name-calling. None specifically directed," Beltron lied.

"Oh, I mean, I would say, 'Son-of-a-bitches, son-of-a-bitch, same situation.' Oh, sure, I mean, that's just me. I probably cuss more than my friends put together. It's just kind of my lingo. I mean, I know it's not right or— Let's put it that way. Right or wrong, I don't know, but it's not good. And that's just the way I, I talk, you know."

"Was it directed at her?"

"Probably the situation," he said. "And, and maybe partly towards her. I, I don't recall now. I, I don't recall. I know just part of the conversation in my mind."

Beltron then asked, "Has your wife ever been up there before?"

"Yes. She's, she's gone up there several times in the last number of years," he said. "I'm not sure what part she goes to per se. It was . . . the ski area and walk around there or if it's downhill further where she was, you know, take a view from down below there and such."

It was another contradiction. Earlier, he called it their favorite spot, then said he'd never gone up there with her before. Now he was saying she had been there, but he didn't know exactly where she had gone.

The interview now was really almost over.

Butko asked, "How much rest have you had?"

"Rest?" asked Peter.

"Yes. Have you even slept at all?"

"Um, if, uh, uh, I mean, I don't know what's, I got back, well, I mean I, I dozed, uh, I don't know, two, three, four hours. I don't know. I feel fine now, you know. I, I, I just know that when I was, I can sit here and swear all day long I was braking that damn car."

"And that's . . ."

Peter interrupted him. "I was braking. I was braking, I was braking, and it was not stopping," he said.

"OK, great, and that's—"

"I mean, I, I, my thing is to get this done, over with."

Beltron said, "Right."

Bergna said, "I want my life back."

"Well, that's what we want to do."

"Yeah."

"We want to get, get you out of the scope of the investigation. That's all."

Butko said, "That, that is the correct way that you want to respond. You're right."

Bergna asked, "What, what, what was, is that?"

"Let's get this thing done and over with, so you can get along."

"That's the way I've always been," said Bergna.

Beltron said, "Um, probably should let you sleep today. Don't you think, Dave?"

Butko said, "I think so. He needs rest."

"Oh, OK," said Bergna.

"You need some rest," Butko told him.

"Yeah, uh, then I can probably do, you know," Bergna said.

Beltron said, "OK."

"So—"

"Nobody here thinks you're a bad guy," said Beltron.

Peter didn't think so either.

"Well, if you looked around town," he said, "you'd find out real quick that I'm a very respected person around town and loved my wife dearly and I'm just sick to, sick to death that I'm going, I'm going to be alone. The one thing I did not want to be is alone. And now I'm alone. It just devastates my life, because, you know, I don't feel it today, 'cause I've got fourteen friends with me I'm with. My parents are coming up, up to Tahoe right now, and the other friends are going to come up and, you know, it's fine now. It's going to— next week when they all leave and I'm home alone by myself. The, the biggest fear is, and I told her that, this, of being home alone."

"That—"

"I do not want to be home alone."

Butko said, "You don't want us calling you and all these other questions and everything."

"Uh-huh."

"You want us out of your life."

That said, Beltron then noted, "Questions are going to come up and if we can get this done and that clears up a lot of questions for us, and it clears it up for you. It gets you out of the scope of our investigation."

So, Beltron asked him, if he didn't mind, would he go down to Reno the next day and take a lie detector test? Nothing major. Just an investigative tool. All very routine.

Bergna said he would. He had nothing to hide. He wanted to do anything he could to cooperate. It was his father's way: truth and justice.

At 12:45 p.m., the officers returned to Bergna the $77.80 in cash found in his wallet and pockets. He signed a receipt acknowledging that he had handed over the clothes and shoes he was wearing during the crash. Then he hobbled out of the substation on crutches and back to a houseful of friends and family, for his first night's sleep in two days.

Chapter 15

It is normal, natural and common for somebody being interviewed by police after a traumatic incident to contradict himself, to ramble, to act in ways—and express emotions—that in other circumstances would be considered inappropriate. Police are used to this and they take it into account. If anything, a calm, clear, coherent narrative from Peter Bergna after a truck crash that had killed his wife—and that could have easily killed him—would have been even more suspicious than one that made total sense.

Still, as Detective James Beltron of the Washoe County Sheriff's Department reviewed his notes following a morning-long grilling of Peter, the cop voice inside him said something was seriously wrong.

As Beltron reconstructed the story, Peter Bergna, a man suffering loneliness and perhaps some anger at his wife for her long time away from him, picks her up at the airport and immediately drives her up to the side of the mountain. A discussion that at times may have been heated centers on the problems in their marriage, including her new job as a tour director and his frustration over their finances. Divorce comes up. Yet Peter insists the conversation ends well enough that the couple will drive a few hundred feet down the hill and pull over to admire the lights of Reno. But somewhere between the end of the road and the turnout, Peter loses control of the truck. The vehicle flies off the mountain with his wife strapped in her seatbelt and crashes hundreds of feet below, killing her. Peter, miraculously, gets out of the truck—somehow—and ends up a short way down the hill, suffering only minor injuries and dialing 911 for help. There are no skid marks, no brake or transmission fluid, no sign at all of a truck that suffered brake, steering or mechanical problems. And Peter himself doesn't know what happened—doesn't even know if he was braking.

The cop voice inside Beltron said this story didn't pass the smell test.

Peter can't explain why he didn't just turn away from the cliff toward the mountain on what was a wide, gentle curve in the road. His explanation for having the two gas cans in the truck—that he needed the extra fuel for a trip to Las Vegas, and to fill up his snow blower and other household machines—strained credibility. And he flat-out contradicted himself on whether his wife had ever even been to that side of the mountain. At one point he said she had—that they enjoyed the romantic view of the lights—but at another point he said she had never been there. Yet Peter had been to that spot just the day before, with the neighbor kids, and was so taken by the altitude and potential danger that he worried about the children getting too close to the edge.

Beltron also was struck by Peter's apparent lack of emotion over his wife's violent death—how he continued to seem irritated by problems in their marriage, even as she lay dead at the morgue. He was the son of a prosecutor and knew that his 911 call would be taped.

Finally, there was the payoff if Rinette died.

Insurance money.

Inheritance.

The demise of a woman causing Peter so much grief would be worth as much as $1 million.

The cop voice inside Beltron couldn't stop asking: Was this murder?

Beltron wasn't the only one suspicious of Peter.

When Peter had finished his interview, there was a group waiting for him at the substation: his parents and Rinette's brothers. Peter greeted them and everyone exchanged bland pleasantries. The group drove separate cars back to the house, Peter in Rick's Expedition because Peter's parents' car, which Rick recalled to be a Jaguar or something like it, was too cramped for Peter to get into with the sprained ankle and crutches. Peter sat in the back of the Expedition for the short drive to the house, then when he got home, went out to the patio and ate a sandwich that somebody had made him.

Rinette's brother Richard Riella struck up a conversation with him—a conversation that quickly steered toward just what had happened the night before up on the mountain. It seemed that Peter was emotionally wrought. He didn't so much as tell the story as blurt it out—"blubbering" was the word Richard used to describe it.

It was essentially the narrative he had laid out for the officers, about how he and Rinette had gone up to the ski area—one of their favorite spots—to work out marital problems. They resolved the most pressing of their issues and decided to drive down to a bend in the road with a view of the valley lights when Peter suddenly couldn't get the brakes to work, and the truck crashed through the guardrail, with Peter thrown through the window and Rinette tumbling to her death.

Richard had known Peter for years, and the explanation struck Richard as odd on a number of levels. But one thing stood out. Bergna had said that while he and his wife were talking, he was smoking a cigar while walking around outside the truck. He didn't stay in the truck, he told Richard, because Rinette didn't like cigar smoke. Yet there were times that Peter and Rinette visited Richard's house and the men would spark up the occasional cigar, and she never complained then. She just told them that smoking was bad for them, but the smoke itself didn't seem to bother her.

Something else seemed strange. At times while telling the story, Peter would break down and make a sort of sobbing sound.

But it was only a sound.

For Peter shed no tears.

Chapter 16

The results of lie detector tests are inadmissible in court in the state of Nevada. The mere mention of the test in front of a jury could be cause for a mistrial. Still, the Washoe County Sheriff's Department, like law enforcement agencies across the country, consider the polygraph a valuable investigative tool. If a detective thinks somebody's lying—or telling the truth—it helps to have some scientific validation, if only to keep the investigation on the right track. There's no use in wasting time on somebody who is obviously innocent—and no good reason to ignore somebody who may be guilty.

In the case of the motor vehicle death of Rinette Riella-Bergna, investigators saw so many problems in Peter Bergna's initial interview that they wanted a more objective gauge of his veracity—to see if the contradictions, selective memory and odd demeanor stemmed from nervousness, injury or emotional trauma from the crash.

Or was he lying to cover a murder?

Investigators knew the polygraph would not be definitive. But it would help them decide what to do next—and how aggressively they would do it.

Peter arrived at the sheriff's station in Reno around 9 a.m. on Tuesday, June 2, 1998, driven by his father Louis Bergna, the former top prosecutor for Santa Clara County. It was now two days after the accident. Peter had the benefit of his first night's sleep. He was led into the polygraph room and introduced to the examiner.

Peter was strapped into the device and asked about the crash.

As he watched the examination over a closed-circuit TV monitor, Detective Beltron was stunned. There were two outcomes that the detective might have expected: Peter would register as truthful, or as lying.

But not this one.

During his examination, Peter disobeyed the instructions of the examiner on how to behave during the questioning. Peter was breathing heavily while talking about the facts surrounding the accident. This threw off the instruments. The examiner told Peter to breathe normally, but still he huffed and puffed.

In the end the examiner couldn't decide whether Peter was lying or not because Peter seemed to be trying to manipulate the test with his heavy breathing.

Beltron needed to talk to Peter again. The detective—convinced that Peter not only was lying, but was devious enough to try to throw off a lie detector test—wanted to pound Peter much harder on what really transpired on the mountain. He wanted to try harder to shake the story that he did give, plunge ever deeper into Bergna's marital problems and, with any luck, score a confession, or at least enough contradictory or damaging information to build a case against him.

The detective asked Peter for a second interview. Surprisingly, Peter agreed.

He even agreed to do it without a lawyer—and without his father, a veteran criminal prosecutor, in the room with him.

Peter's hubris seemed to know no bounds. And that was OK with Beltron.

Sure enough, as Peter sat in the interview chair, for a session that this time would be videotaped, he seemed to Beltron to be even more arrogant and self-centered than the day before, and, amazingly, showed even less concern for what had happened to his wife.

"You said she is a doctor of pharmacy?" Beltron asked.

"If I say this right, I'll be lucky," said Bergna, his voice dripping with false modesty. "She's a doctor of pharmacy with a PhD. I think that's what it is. . . . The way she tells me this, it's different."

"She's an educated person?"

"Sure."

"Did she work in a pharmacy?"

"Good question, too," Bergna said. He then gave some advice to his questioner: "Now, you've got to do this in time frame because she was all over the place with this stuff, OK? So, I mean, yes, she worked in pharmacies. . . . She was dispensing medication at the request of people who wanted to take vacations. Does that make sense? She was not dispensing medications anymore on a full-time vacation."

"So she's kind of a pharmacy sitter?"

"OK, right," said Bergna.

Beltron asked about Rinette's career.

"She did a complete turnaround career change," said Bergna, with a befuddled tone to his voice.

"Tell me about that."

"I'll give you a quote from her brother: 'Rinette got excited going to an airport.' "

"She liked to travel?"

"She liked to travel. The woman loved to travel. She loved to travel. Her thing in life was to go travel. . . . She was a tour director."

And on went the interview, covering much of the same ground as the day before: Peter, the lonely husband of an absentee wife, goes up the mountain with her and only one comes back alive. And he has no idea how the accident happened. The benefit of sleep only seemed to give Peter more confidence. He gave an even rosier picture of how the discussion on the mountain went—saying Rinette totally saw things his way, totally understood his concerns. And, even though she had just come back from a long trip from Europe, it was the middle of the night, Rinette was full of energy.

"Remember now, for her it's morning now," Peter reminded Beltron. "She's waking up. She'll go on four hours of sleep a night. Four hours for her, bing, bing, 'Here we go, folks, let's go and see the world.' "

"A lot of energy, huh?"

With a what-a-gal tone, Bergna said, "Boy, she had a lot of energy. She loved it. She was never at a loss for a dull moment. And he insisted he didn't fool around when she was gone.

"That's not your bag?" Beltron asked.

"I never cheated on my wife. I never cheated on my first wife, and when we were going through a divorce and I could have gone out if I wanted to, and I didn't do that. I stayed home. And people think that's stupid and that's not right."

But still, the circumstances of the crash eluded Peter.

And then, for the first time, Peter was overcome by emotion. His voice breaking, he said: "I'm thinking to myself. I'm thinking, 'If I can't stop, I'm losing my life and she loses her life. I'm in control here. I'm the one who's supposed to be stopping this thing, and I can't stop it, I can't.' " His voice cracked. "I don't know why I won't stop. I tried to stop the car. And then it won't stop, and I don't know why it won't stop, I don't know why it won't stop."

He sobbed for a moment, then stopped.

Beltron never offered him a tissue.

He didn't see any tears.

Then, as quickly as he was struck by emotion, Bergna recovered.

"You have to understand," he said. "I drive twenty-five thousand to thirty-five thousand miles a year with my job. I'm on the road. I'm all over the place. I drive all the time, and I couldn't get the car to stop."

Then he broke down again with dry sobs.

"And it didn't stop! Why didn't it stop? I drive so much. I drive all the time. I'm a good driver. I never crashed in years and years, and it didn't stop, and I don't know why it didn't stop!"

"Somehow you got out of the truck?"

"Somehow I got out of the truck."

"But you don't recall?"

"I don't know if I opened the door," he said. "I don't remember if I jumped out, threw out, ran out, opened the door."

"Where you ended up was down below the guardrail. So, can we probably assume that you were still in the truck when it went through the guardrail?"

Bergna then became testy. "You can assume anything you want. I can't help you here. I can't help you. I wish I had an answer. I wish I could tell you, 'Yeah, I went through the guardrail and I opened the door and jumped out through the door.' "

Asking Bergna about his frame of mind, Beltron asked, "When you picked Rinette up at the airport, at that point in time, there was no thought in your mind about any ill will?"

"You know what was on my mind?" Peter gave Beltron a knowing guy grin.

"You wanted to go home and get laid," the detective stated.

"Exactly," said Bergna. "I had gone to a party with all my friends, Incline High School Boosters, and my joke there—and I'm a very open person, they know this—'Don't call me for the next two days. I want to get laid.' I said, 'Don't call me. I'll be busy here, folks.' I love sex. I love my wife. I love to touch my wife. That's what I wanted to do was go home and have sex with her. I even thought about doing it on top of the mountain. I came real close. My wife would have freaked out. I knew that. I was going to bring up the towels and the lotions and the whole thing, we'll talk for a while, and work some things out and so forth, and make love on the mountain. To me, it would be fabulous. To her, no. She wanted to go home and do it at home. She wanted to go home and do it home." Bergna sighed. "She wanted to go home and do it at home."

"Her death was not deliberate on your part?"

It was the first time Beltron had confronted Peter with a murder accusation. Peter didn't flinch.

"Not in any way, form or fashion," he said, his voice full of confidence.

This would have completed Beltron's questioning of Bergna but for one thing that happened. After the interview, at the elevators, Bergna was standing next to his father, and Beltron was just a few feet away.

That's when he heard Bergna tell his father: "I did it."

Chapter 17

"I'm not trying to sit here and bamboozle you."

Detective Beltron was setting the tone. This wasn't an interrogation. Bergna wasn't under arrest. He wasn't read his rights. His father, a legendary attorney, was now at his side.

Bergna picked up on the new serious tone. "I'm the best at my job, you're the best at your job," he told the detective.

The battle lines were drawn.

"Like I said, my thing is: We just left downstairs, and as we leave, we see your dad," said Beltron. "I ask for thirty minutes for an interview with you, and while you're talking to him, you say, 'You know, I did it.' And I'd like to know what it is that you did?"

"I loved my wife," Bergna said.

"I understand."

"Please understand my position in this whole thing," said Peter, not answering the question. "I lose my wife.

My feeling is, four guys coming to my house. Four guys. How would you feel if four guys came here and pulled you out of your house? One guy came, or two guys came, I would have said, 'You know what? No problem, I understand, it has to be done.' I've been in the criminal justice business my whole life with my father. I've seen it happen every day for years. I'm being treated like a criminal here. All my friends tell me, 'Go get an attorney.' Guys, back off here. I don't need an attorney. I didn't do anything wrong here. I loved my wife. I wanted to take her home and seduce her."

"I don't doubt that for a minute."

"How would you feel if four guys came to your house and pulled you out? Not one, not two, four. Four men. Would you be a little concerned there at that point? I think I would be."

"It was voluntarily."

"Sure it was voluntarily. You don't need four men to come pull me out."

"I don't think we pulled you out. We asked you if you want to come down there. Let's get back to my question: What is it that you did that you are admitting to your dad?"

"I've admitted to nothing," Bergna said. "I did nothing wrong. I did nothing wrong. You guys think I'm guilty. I know that for a fact. I know that. It's obvious."

"What do we think you're guilty of?"

"Of killing my wife. You think that since I loved my wife, I killed my wife. I loved my wife. That's all there is to it."

"I don't doubt that you do love her. I just think some things happened up there that got out of hand. You're not a bad guy."

"Yeah."

"You're not a bad guy, are you?"

"God almighty! I have never touched my wife, except to make love to her, or to help her. Ever. Ever! My wife would never stand for that. I wanted to make love to her, period. That was it. We talked about, when we left the first spot and came down the second spot, she agreed with me that she was going to stay home, and maybe go out for a couple weeks. She was making me happy. Why would I want to kill her now? It doesn't make any sense to me."

"You're the only one who knows that answer. I can't answer that question."

"I've been trying, sir, for two days to tell you guys this stuff. I'm under a microscope, so to speak, for hours with you guys, telling you what I know. I wanted to make love to my wife, not kill my wife. She told me what I wanted to hear. I was not going to be alone anymore at home, which is what I had feared. And now I'm alone at home. The one thing I do not want in this whole thing was to be alone. Now I'm alone. I don't understand."

"So there was a mistake? It was an accident?"

"There was no mistake. I don't understand what you mean by mistake."

"You didn't mean to do it. Is that what you're saying?"

"I'm sorry?"

"You didn't mean to do it?"

"Mean to do—" Bergna had exasperation in his voice, like he'd had to tell this tale one time too many. "My mind is telling me I'm braking, I'm not braking. I'm panicking, I'm not braking. But my mind is telling me I'm braking, but I'm not braking. We're still moving. You heard me saying here, I drive twenty-five thousand, thirty-five thousand miles a year, for the last fifteen years. You figure it out mileage-wise. I'm a good driver. I know for a fact when I drive, I'm a good driver. I know I'm a fast driver. I understand that. She would have told you the same thing."

"But she can't."

"I understand that. And I'm the one who has to go to bed tonight by myself, in my bed, by myself, and know that she's not going to be next to me. I understand all that. And the one thing I didn't want in this whole damn thing was to be alone, and now I'm alone. I wanted her to stay home with me. That was the whole point of the conversation on the hill. I wanted her to stay home with me. You go up to Incline Village, and anybody in Incline Village will tell you what I talked about when she was gone for six weeks: I was tired of being alone. I didn't want to be alone. I wanted to be with somebody."

"I could understand that."

"I don't think you do. If you did, you'd understand what I'm telling you is the truth. I have no reason. There is no reason in any form or fashion why I would kill my wife. Talk to my wife? Work things out in my marriage? Who doesn't?"

"I believe what you said. I think you're a nice guy. I think you're a good guy. I think it was a spur-of-the-moment thing. I don't think it was any grandiose plan. Right downstairs, you admitted it to your dad."

"No, I admitted to my father what you guys are trying to do to me. And this is why everybody told me 'Hire an attorney' before I came down here. 'Go get an attorney.' "

"Isn't this part of the truth?"

"I don't understand your question."

"You know, you always said your dad raised you to tell the truth?"

"That is correct."

"And I think now is the time to start."

"If you tell me that one more time, I'm going to walk out of here, because I've been telling you from day one, from day one, I've been telling you the truth. And if you can't believe that, I have nothing more to tell you. There's no more I can tell you. I've been telling you the truth from day one. I've been telling you the truth from day one. I don't know what to tell you anymore. I told you, I'm going down the road, I'm putting my foot on the brake, I think I'm braking, my mind's telling me I'm braking, but the car's not stopping. I don't know what else to tell you."

"What about the steering? Could you turn away from there?"

"Yes you can. I didn't, did I?"

"No."

"Didn't I? I brake, I brake. I didn't steer. I broke."

"Your wife, who wears the seatbelt religiously, is suddenly unseatbelted?"

This was another curveball question. Beltron knew she was in her seatbelt. Peter also knew it.

"No way!" Bergna barked. "She was seatbelted in that car. I know for a fact she was seatbelted. I know for a fact she was seatbelted in that car. She was seatbelted." Bergna, anger and disgust in his face, started to get up, rattling around with his crutches. "You're trying to set me up with this one. You're setting me up. I can't believe it. I cannot get through this thing. You guys are setting me up. I can't believe it. She was seatbelted in that car."

And with that, Bergna hobbled away in apparent anger.

The interview appeared to be over. Peter's cooperation had ended. There was the very real possibility that this was the last time investigators would ever talk to him.

But then something happened.

Within minutes, Peter was back in the interview room.

He had spoken to his father. What they said would never be known, but whatever it was, it got Peter back in there—a new, contrite Peter.

It was an incredible opportunity. For whatever reason, Peter's father—who, as a prosecutor, knew fully well the dangers of even innocent people talking to police without a lawyer present—was apparently giving his tacit approval to do just that.

The detective didn't want to risk losing a word of it in court.

"As you know, we make no bones about the camera being visible," he told Bergna.

"I understand," Peter said quietly.

"Last time you left, you left because you wanted to."

"That is correct."

"I have to cover this, obviously, for a wide variety of reasons. You're here because you want to be. I didn't drag you back in here?"

"I understand that. That is correct."

"You didn't get forced by anybody who works here or works for us to come back to the building?"

"No, I did not."

"There ain't no threats or promises?"

"Nothing."

"OK. I just want to make sure."

"I know, I know."

"Like I said, you're free to walk right back out that door again, OK? I don't want you to think this is anything more than what it is."

"I know."

"Now as we last left, we were talking about the seatbelt."

"Right."

"You claimed she wore it religiously, and all I said was, the seatbelt wasn't on her when we found her."

"You're correct, and as I was thinking about it, maybe she was trying to get out and trying to unhook it and get out. I apologize for being upset, because I was wrong."

"There are some things I *do* know about the truck."

"OK."

"And I'm not going to tell you everything I know about the truck."

"I understand that."

"There are some things I know about your wife. Some of those things you don't *need* to know."

It was Beltron's hint: Rinette died in a horrible way.

"I understand," said Peter.

"I'm not going to tell you."

"I understand."

"I'm certainly not going to show you pictures. The pictures I have you don't want to see."

"I know."

"OK?"

"I know."

"OK, now, I'm not politically correct, and I say what's on my mind."

"I understand that."

"I'm here after the truth."

"I understand that."

"OK, and that's what it's all about."

"I understand."

"The thing is, I get paid to do a job. I'm doing my job."

"I understand that."

"I don't exchange Christmas cards with a lot of people, and it doesn't hurt my feelings."

"I understand that, too."

"OK, that's something I live with. I've never met you before. I don't have any preconceived ideas of you."

"I understand."

"OK, all I look at is the facts. And the truth. And right now I'm not hearing it, and all I'd like to do is hear the truth from you."

"OK."

"That's what I'm here after, is the truth. And there's acceptance of responsibility, OK? We all do things. The acceptance of responsibility for what we do is important, OK? So what I'd like to do is hear the truth from you as to what happened, OK? Your dad asked to sit in here. Absolutely I can deny it."

"I understand that."

"And he doesn't have anything in his hands to force you to say something you don't want to say."

"I'm an adult. I understand that."

And then Louis Bergna made his first comment of the interview. He told his son, "And he wants you to tell the truth, Peter."

"He" being Beltron.

It was as if there were a second police interviewer in the room—Peter's own father.

"I understand that, Father. I understand that," said Peter.

Beltron said, "The whole idea here is that I don't have any preconceived ideas of you, again, OK?"

"I understand."

"The fact is, what I'm hearing doesn't match what I'm seeing."

"I understand."

"I am not an accident reconstructionist. Some things happened up there that need to be told to me that haven't been told to me yet. They can only come from you."

"I understand that."

"Because you're the only one alive that's left there to say that."

"I totally understand that."

"But you have to be aware that there are other things coming in all the time. When they're reviewing the truck, they'll be going over it with a fine-toothed comb. They can reconstruct the truck."

"I understand that."

"Bit by bit, piece by piece, that fell off as it went over."

"I understand that."

"So all I'm asking for is the truth, OK?"

"I agree. I agree."

"OK, but so far, just from what I know about what happened, I haven't heard the truth. I'd like to hear the truth from you. So do you want to start? At the beginning is probably the best place."

"Do you want me to tell you that I feel like it's my fault, that I did something wrong up on the hill?"

"Yes, I do."

"I understand that."

"OK," said Beltron.

"I know I did, I did something wrong up there," said Bergna, but if Beltron thought he was going to get a murder confession, he was wrong. "I didn't do what probably could have been done to stop this vehicle. Whether I was hitting the gas pedal or the brake, I don't know. I can't tell you. Do I feel like I did something wrong? Damn right I feel like I did something wrong. Do you think I'm guilty up there? I feel like I'm guilty up there. I know I did something wrong. Did I do it on purpose? There's no way in hell I'd do anything on purpose up there. There's no way that I would ever kill my wife, there's no reason whatsoever. I don't care how bad anything could ever get at home, you don't kill anybody. You just don't do that. Did I do something wrong up on the hill up there? You bet I did. I killed my wife. I did something wrong with the driving. I made a mistake. But I can't tell you if I was hitting the brake or the gas pedal. I don't know. I don't remember. . . . Why didn't I turn the car? I was focused on hitting the brake, and my mind has always told me, in three hundred thousand, four hundred thousand miles of driving a car, if you hit the brake, you're going to stop. No problem. Am I guilty? Do I feel like I'm guilty? I feel like I'm guilty. Yes, I feel like I did something wrong. There's no question about that."

Bergna continued in this vein, admitting his "guilt" to "doing something wrong," but not intentionally, and whatever it was he did wrong, he couldn't remember.

"How did you leave the vehicle?" Beltron asked, but again the answer—or non-answer—would be the same: "I don't know."

Instead, Bergna rambled about how he would have to live with this the rest of his life, how nobody will trust him to drive their kids around anymore. He began to sob again, dry sobs like before, saying, "I know that, I know I'm a good driver, and I know I did something wrong. I'm wrong. I know I'm wrong up there. I'm not trying to hide. If you think that, they would have talked to me down at the station, that I was trying to hide the fact that I did something wrong up on the hill. Maybe I'm thinking that I purposely killed her. There's no way in hell I'd ever do that to anybody. There's no way. That's not me. Not even for an instant would I think I would want to kill somebody."

On and on he went, saying that he was up there to make love to her, not kill her, "The God's honest truth," but that forever there would be "guilt on my shoulders" that he could do nothing about.

"I know that. I have to go down and face her family. Her family here, her family in Italy still. And they're going to think I'm guilty for the rest of my life, whether they believe it or not. They're going to think, 'Gee, maybe, did he want to do something up there or not?' "

"You're the only one who can answer that question, other than what we can reconstruct," said Beltron.

"And I'm trying to tell you the truth. I did everything I thought possible to do at the time. I did everything I thought possible I could do. I know that I'm wrong. I know I am. You're wrong when something happens, then you have to take responsibility for it. I've been taught all my life: Tell the truth, take responsibility, and that's all I've ever done in my life. I tell the truth, I take responsibility for it. And in this case, I'm wrong. I know I'm wrong. I know I'm guilty of doing it because I didn't stop it."

The interview then took another nasty turn when Beltron said he had found women's shoeprints at the scene and suggested that Bergna was lying when he said she never got out of the car.

"No sir, no siree. Not even close, Jim. Don't remember her getting out of the car. There is no way in hell, that's my wife," he said. Adding that the only place he walked was in the pavement. Later, it would emerge that Peter's frustration had some basis. It was never shown conclusively that those footprints did belong to Rinette or Peter.

"I'm not worried about that one," said Peter. "I know I'm not walking in the dirt."

Then Bergna made an allegation against Beltron.

"You've got [my] shoes. I know you do. And tell me this: I think you're an honest person, but what's stopping you from going up there, making footprints in the dirt with my shoes and say, 'Oh, here it is, here are the photographs'?"

"Why would I do that?" Beltron asked.

"I don't know. But that's what I'm thinking. I know myself. I ain't walking in the dirt."

"We didn't have your shoes until after the photographs were taken."

The pictures were taken the night of the crash. The shoes were seized the next morning at the interview. Bergna had signed a receipt. Suddenly, he was no longer accusing Beltron. Bergna was back to the contrite demeanor he had shown earlier, apologizing profusely and insisting he simply didn't remember certain key events, like how he had gotten out of the car. Beltron then went back on the offensive.

"Have you ever had any blackouts before?" Beltron asked him.

"Not that I know of."

"Have you had any blackouts since?"

"Not that I remember, no."

"I think you do know. I just don't think you want to say it."

"That I blacked out?"

"No, I think you do know how you got out of the truck. You just don't want to say it."

"I don't know how I got out of the truck, Jim. I wish I knew how I got out of the truck. I'm alive. I should be grateful to be alive. And go on from there. I may have opened the door, for all I know, and jumped out of the truck. I don't know. I may have jumped out of the window. I don't know."

"If that's what happened, that's what I would like to hear."

"But if I can sit here and tell you, 'Jim, I was panicking, I opened the door, I jumped out, I rolled down the hill,' I would say that's what I did. I don't know. I can't tell you what I don't know. I can only tell you what I recall."

Beltron then drew a picture on a piece of paper, sketching out a diagram of the accident scene, showing him how his explanation of faulty brakes just didn't make sense.

"This is the cliffside. The rocks. This is the guardrail. There's a sign here. A windsock. What we have is a straight line, straight to that section . . . where a simple turn of the wheel would have pulled you away from it. A simple turn of the wheel would have pulled you into this lane."

"I understand that, too."

"I'd like to find out what happened that caused it that you couldn't turn."

"First of all, when I'm coming down here, I'm thinking I'm going to stop here and park, with my nose up against this thing, where you get out of the car and look at the lights."

"Sure."

"So there's no reason for me to think about turning. I'm going to go right to it. By the time I realized I can't stop, I'm panicked. I'm too late. I can't turn. I can't do anything. I'm thinking about doing one thing: stopping. My intention was to go straight. There's no question about that. Stop right here, get out, look at the lights."

"I understand the fact there's no attempt to stop. I understand that," said Beltron.

At this point, Bergna's father made a rare correction. "You mean no attempt to turn, don't you, Jim?"

"Or stop," said Beltron. "There's nothing to show anything. There's no attempt to turn, no attempt to stop, there's nothing in the roadway."

"I understand that," said Peter Bergna.

"I *don't* understand it," said the detective.

"In my mind, I'm braking as hard as I can."

Beltron tried another tack, suggesting that the absence

of evidence didn't look good for Bergna. For one thing, he told him, the airbag should have burst open when the truck hit the guardrail. If Bergna were still in the truck at the time, and didn't jump out before it went over the cliff, his clothes should have been covered in the white cornstarch powder used to lubricate airbags as they inflate. Instead, his jacket and shirt showed no obvious signs of the powder, although it was still being tested microscopically.

"The airbag should have deployed. You should have known it," he said. What's more, the detective suggested, why was Bergna only thirty feet down the hill?

This seemed to throw him.

"What you're saying is I was only thirty feet down?"

"About." It was actually closer to eighty feet; Beltron was fudging again. "And the only injury you have is a twisted ankle. People leave, they're going to land on their hands."

"You've been to that hill?" asked Bergna.

"Yes, I have. I climbed it yesterday."

"You walked down there and so forth?"

"I went down."

"It's sand. Sand. I was in sand. I was eating sand last night. I had sand in my hair. I had sand in the gurney. Sand in the hospital. Sand on my face. Sand in my mouth."

"But it's not all sand."

"Well . . ."

"Manzanita and a lot of rocks and boulders."

"Rocks and boulders, yes there are, there's no question," acknowledged Bergna. "I've got a bruise here and I've got a bruise on my hip here and so forth. All I can tell you is, I was eating sand the whole time I was going down that hill. There's no question about that one. If what you're saying is, if I would have jumped out on the pavement, I'd be scratched up, bruised up, everything else hitting that pavement whatever speed I was going at. There's no way."

Beltron said he thought the car had to be going 40 to 50 mph to make it through the barrier.

"There's no way I was going that fast," said Bergna.

"I'm just saying, forty to fifty miles per hour, the truck goes through, lands down here—but you land here, but you're going the same speed as the truck."

"There's no way, there's no way I was going forty to fifty miles per hour. There's no way I was going that fast. There's no way. There's no way."

"How fast *were* you going?"

"I was not going forty to fifty miles per hour, I know that much. I know speeds pretty well. I'm on the road a lot. I know my speeds. If I was going twenty, twenty-five miles per hour, at the maximum, at the max. There's no way."

"If we put your car at twenty-five miles per hour, it doesn't make it through there. That makes you a liar."

"Sure does. I understand that. I understand that. I'm going forty or fifty miles per hour? No. Thirty-five miles per hour? No way. I don't believe that. I don't believe that whatsoever. There's no way."

"Certainly you would land a lot closer to the vehicle if you left the vehicle at the same speed it went through?"

"Yeah, no question about that, too. And there's no question that if I'm hitting the accelerator instead of the brake, and my mind's thinking I'm hitting the brake but I'm hitting the accelerator, yeah, maybe I could be going forty miles per hour. As far as I knew, I didn't think I was going that fast."

"Don't get me wrong, I'm not an accident reconstructionist."

"I understand that, too."

"But I've had basic physics, and I've had basic chemistry and the rest."

"I understand what you're saying."

"These are questions I have to have answers to. You don't recall this, you don't remember that, you don't recall this, you don't remember that. It's not making sense to me."

"I explained to you that I take responsibility for what I did. I know I did it. I know I'm guilty for that. Whether I hit the brake or the gas, I don't remember. I don't remember. Listen to the 911 tape. I'm yelling for my wife. I'm in pain where I am, I'm screaming for my wife."

"It doesn't make sense. Physically, it can't happen that way. If you're in the vehicle, physically it can't happen. I mean, it doesn't make sense. It's mathematically—the laws of probability—incorrect. Power of inertia. Objects in motion tend to stay in motion, unless acted upon by another force."

"I don't understand that, but that's OK."

"I *do*," said Beltron.

"I don't."

"That's the whole idea here. I'm trying to make it as simple as I can. My drawings are pretty simple."

"I appreciate that. Thank you."

"That's because I'm pretty simple. It has to be simple for me to understand it. But there are things I do understand."

"But I also understand this: If your theory is correct, you say I'm going forty-five to fifty miles per hour, I'm jumping out of a car before it goes over, I'm hurting myself," said Peter. "I'm going to run into that gate or guard— Whatever it is. I'm going to be scratched up, scraped up, hit the guard and so forth. I'm going to stop right on top of the hill there. I understand that."

"What's the other alternative? You weren't in the truck. And you jumped over the side."

"The window was open. I could have gone out the window for all I know. I don't know. I can't tell you what I don't know."

Beltron stopped his questions and asked if anybody wanted anything to drink. Bergna asked for a Diet Pepsi or water. His father asked if Beltron needed any quarters for the machine, but the detective said he had drinks. When he returned with the sodas, everybody was trying to make peace.

Louis Bergna said, "You asked for a half-hour and I've given you over an hour and a half."

"Well," said Beltron, "I was just going to come back in here and say you fellas have been real cooperative."

"We want to be," said Louis Bergna.

"I apologize for any kind of differences we may have had," said Beltron. "I want to make sure that you understand the door is free and open. I intended to come in and say we'd rather depart friends. What it is, there's a lot of other things that come in. I've talked to you a lot. I'm not going to sit and not going to browbeat you. I'm not going to raise my voice. I'm not going to."

"It's not a matter of friendship," said Louis Bergna, "but if you would like another twenty minutes or a half-hour, if you would, we'll give it to you."

"You guys have had a long day. All right. So why don't we just do it this way: I'm obviously going to need to talk to you again after the truck is processed and some other things."

"I understand," said Peter Bergna.

"If you have anything, you have my phone numbers."

"If we have any thoughts on the matter," said Louis Bergna, "God knows you'll know we're thinking about it. We'll get ahold of you."

"I don't expect this is going to leave anybody any

time soon," the detective said. "I just need to make sure, like you said, the thing is, excuse the expression, but I'm not going to beat this up. I'm not going to beat you up."

Peter Bergna said he understood. "Listen, I do investigations every day of my life. It's like you in a different sense. I'm looking for information around the world to appraise an antique piece of furniture," he said. "I understand that. But I understand what you're doing. I do this every single day. I'm an investigator of my own. I have to sit there and understand why this is worth X amount of dollars and be able to walk into a court of law and prove why, through a third party, which is the judge, why this piece of paper is worth ten thousand dollars and tell him why. Sometimes I can't do it, sometimes I can do it. I do the best job I can. But I understand. I'm looking at books. I'm talking to friends. Talking to people. It's the same thing I do in my job. So I understand what you're doing. But when it gets emotional—and me, I'm an actual person—and a loss and so forth and so on, I don't handle it very well. I understand that."

"Like you said, I think we're done for today," said the detective. "You've had an awful long day. I'm not going to sit here and tell you you've got to stay any longer. You wanted a half an hour, you gave it to me, I appreciate that."

"I gave you three times what you asked for," said Bergna. "And I'll do one better right now. If you want another half an hour, I'll give you another half an hour right now. I have no problem with that."

"I don't see any reason to stay here any further."

"Except I can't use my crutches and drink my Coke at the same time. Now, that's a problem for me," said Bergna. He said it in a joking way.

"That's part of the trick," Beltron said.

Louis Bergna laughed.

"Aha," said Peter Bergna, "now he tried to trip me up now, Dad."

"You saw right through that, didn't he?" said the detective.

"Yeah," said Bergna.

"Six hours and ten minutes, non-stop," said Peter. "Now I've been here six hours and forty-five minutes. I can keep track of time. It's my business. I bill by the hour."

"I wish I could bill by the hour," said Beltron.

Things became so chummy that Louis Bergna told an anecdote.

"I can remember many, many times—and I'm sure you can, too, [Peter]—when I would go to the theater with my wife and be watching a movie and right in the middle of the movie I would excuse myself and go out to the front of the theater and take out my notebook and write down a couple of questions I thought that I wanted to use on the case I was filing that day," he said. "I'd have the case with me twenty-four hours a day, like you say."

"You don't forget about things like this," agreed Beltron.

"Then you have thirty-six- and forty-eight-hour days," said Louis Bergna.

"That's right. That's right," said Beltron.

"Thank you, Jim," said Louis Bergna.

"I apologize for getting upset," said Peter Bergna. "I really do."

"You're not doing anything wrong to hurt me," said Beltron.

And with that, father and son talked about stopping at

McDonald's on the way back to the house in Incline Village, then left the sheriff's station. They were all on good terms, ending with Lou Bergna's little speech and Peter Bergna's apology.

Police would never interview Peter again.

Chapter 18

On Wednesday, June 3, 1998, the day after Peter Bergna and his father Louis wrapped up the last in the series of interviews with authorities, the local newspaper, the *Reno Gazette-Journal,* ran this short article:

> **One killed after crash through guard rail**
> RENO — A pickup crashed through a guard rail along the Mount Rose Highway and rolled more than 700 feet down an embankment near Slide Mountain early Monday. The wreck killed the passenger and injured the driver.
>
> Peter Bergna, 46, Incline Village, was thrown from the vehicle after he drove through the guardrail on state Route 431.
>
> He fell about 50 feet.
>
> He telephoned the Nevada Highway Patrol to report the accident at about 12:15 a.m. Monday, the patrol said.
>
> Rinette Riella-Bergna, 49, of Incline Village

was reported dead at the scene of the truck. Peter Bergna was flown to Washoe County Medical Center, where he was treated for minor injuries and released.

The state patrol and Washoe County sheriff's office were investigating the accident, and toxicology reports were pending, the patrol said.

The article offered no hint of authorities' unease with Bergna's story from the interviews—indeed, as far as the public knew, there were no interviews. The crash made hardly a ripple in the valley cities of Reno and Carson City. Another one bites the dust on a mountain road.

Authorities also didn't take any dramatic action. Despite the signs of manipulating the polygraph and despite the fact that Beltron all but accused Bergna of being a murderer based on the answers he gave during the interviews, Bergna was not arrested in his wife's death the day that story appeared, or the next day, or the next. Rather, investigators decided to keep him free while continuing with their work. Although they had plenty of suspicions, there was still no hard evidence that Bergna had murdered his wife. There were no witnesses, no confession, no conclusive physical evidence at the scene. Just a mangled truck and a story that seemed fishy. Beltron was awaiting more evidence.

One of the first things that Beltron wanted to see were the results of the autopsy on Rinette Riella-Bergna. A medical examiner could possibly tell whether she had been killed before the crash—by gunshot, knifing, or blow to the head, for instance—then sent off the cliff in the truck as cover for the accident. The fact that Peter Bergna had two gas cans in the back of the truck, recently filled up, along with the tank, could have indicated that he'd wanted the truck to blow up in the crash, obliterating any evidence of how Rinette was really killed.

Dr. Roger S. Ritzlin conducted the autopsy at the Washoe County Coroner's Office in Reno. After removing Rinette's body from the blue bag, Ritzlin observed superficial scrapes and bruises, including scrapes to her stomach and neck from the seatbelt. During the internal examination, Ritzlin found how severely Rinette was hurt: thirteen broken ribs—ten on the right side, three on the left—a broken right wrist, and a broken right kneecap. Both of her collarbones were dislocated. Blood had flowed into her chest cavity. Her head was severely injured, with swelling and bleeding to the brain. And her neck was snapped. The official cause of death: multiple injuries due to blunt force trauma. There were no other signs of trauma from a weapon, and no signs of any poison. Ritzlin said he simply couldn't tell whether the fatal injuries—the broken neck and head trauma—were inflicted before or during the crash. If Peter Bergna had killed his wife, then sent her off the cliff to make it look like an accident, this autopsy examination would not provide the answer.

The next development in the investigation was more promising for authorities. A helicopter had been called in to lift the truck wreckage from the side of the mountain and fly it down to Reno, where the truck made its way onto cinderblocks in the garage of Dewey Dean Willie, who was in charge of maintaining the mechanical integrity of the Nevada Highway Patrol northern command's 230 units, changing the tires, fixing the brakes, lubing the chases. He also was in charge of inspecting vehicles involved in fatal accidents, performing the automotive equivalent of an autopsy, poking around with his screwdrivers and wrenches for clues to the cause of the

crash. It would be up to Willie to determine whether
there was any evidence in the truck wreckage to help
corroborate—or refute—Bergna's claims that he was hitting the brakes and nothing happened.

On Friday, June 5, 1998, at 11:30 a.m., he inspected
the 1997 Ford F-150 XLT 4x4 with 23,452 miles on it.
For all intents and purposes, Peter Bergna had been driving a new truck. Willie looked at the transmission, engine, drive train, tires, brakes, steering and suspension,
searching for components not damaged by the crash, but
broken or malfunctioning beforehand. If a component appeared to have been faulty or missing before the crash,
that area of the car would be photographed and the information written down in the report. It wasn't easy to see
everything. The truck was a mess by the time it ended up
in Willie's garage. The left rear back tire and its brakes
were missing; they'd apparently ended up somewhere on
that steep slope and were never found.

Out of this wreckage, a story emerged—indications of
what had happened up on the mountain, much of it actually corroborating Bergna's account. The driver's side
window was in the rolled-down position, just as Bergna
said it had been, because, he said, he was smoking a cigar. The glass was all shattered inside the door. There was
a cell phone holder in the truck, also as Bergna had said.
The gear shift was in drive position, though Willie
couldn't determine whether the truck was in drive when it
went off the cliff or whether the gear shift had gone into
that position during the crash. Bergna should have had no
problem seeing the roadway. The filaments in the head-
lamps were intact and the headlight switch was on. The
right turn signal was on—raising the grotesque possibility that he signaled out of habit before turning right into
the guardrail—but the signal switch easily could have

moved in the crash, Willie believed. The parking lights were on, the emergency lights were off. The windshield wipers were off, and—though Bergna had complained about the cold night—the heater and defrosters were off and the fan was set on low. The air-conditioning was off, and the radio/tape player was turned on. Willie's report didn't mention what station. As for the airbags, Willie confirmed that the driver's-side bag in the steering wheel had inflated, but that the passenger-side bag in the dash had not, having been deactivated by a manual switch, again as Bergna had said they were.

The more critical issue was the condition of the brakes and steering. Willie pulled off the tires, the power brake drums and the disc brake calipers for inspection. This truck had what is called a duel stage master cylinder, a safety feature that splits the brake system into front and back systems. If a brake line gets cut in the front and the front brakes go out, that wouldn't affect the back brakes, and vice-versa. Willie found that the brake lines were intact. The brake pads and linings also were within safe zones. The brakes were in such good condition that Bergna shouldn't have heard so much as a squeak, much less lost all ability to stop the truck.

Still, just to be sure, Willie also checked the truck's maintenance history in the files of Jones West Ford and found no history of any brake problems—just routine oil and filter changes and replacement of something called an EGO sensor, an exhaust gas oxygen sensor, on May 7, 1998. The garage had also fixed a mirror switch and tinkered with the transmission. None of this would have affected Bergna's ability to stop the truck. "There was," Willie would conclude, "no problem with the brakes."

Although Bergna had said he didn't even try to veer away from the guardrail, Willie checked the steering system—the tie end rods, the steering knuckles—and again everything was intact, not even broken by the car's tumbling down the cliff. The hydraulic steering fluid line had not been cut.

This wouldn't be the end of the investigation of the truck. Ford would have to be contacted to determine whether this truck model was prone to brake problems of the sort that Willie couldn't detect in his garage. Also, Ford would have to get involved in the examination of the airbag. As Beltron had brought up during the interview, airbags generally are lubricated by a white talcum-powder–type substance that would leave a passenger covered in dust after an accident. Bergna didn't seem to have had any dust on his clothing, raising the question of whether he'd jumped out of the truck *before* it hit the guardrail and triggered the airbag, sending out the cloud of dust into an empty driver's side of the cab. Had Bergna been thrown through the window after the guardrail strike, he should have had at least some dust on him, not to mention considerably more injuries. The clothes were sent out for examination—it was possible the dust was there but just not visible. It was also possible that this model of Ford didn't use as much powder, or used a different kind of lubricant, that Beltron had seen in other accidents. Ford would have to provide that answer, and that would take some time.

In all, much work remained before a decision on an arrest could be made. In truth, while this accident probe was starting to tilt toward a homicide investigation—though nobody was calling it that—investigators felt no urgency. There were no witnesses to the crash who could disappear or change their minds, and Bergna didn't seem like a flight risk. From all investigators could tell, Bergna was the model citizen of Incline Village that he claimed to be. They would just wait and see how the investigation unfolded and what Bergna did and said. Detectives would try to bring him in for yet another interview—the man did seem to like to talk, and the more he talked the more he tended to get himself into trouble. Maybe, investigators hoped, Bergna would make a mistake.

Chapter 19

Much of the time, in the days and weeks after the crash, Peter Bergna was in a daze. His employee Adelaide Gramanz took over the day-to-day operations of his business. His friend Mark Steven Sampson saw Peter from Sunday night through the following Tuesday. "Two days before I was leaving for the World Cup in France, I went to Reno to see him. He was depressed. He was distraught. I've never seen him cry. In fact, when his grandfather died—and I know that he was very close to this grandfather—I didn't see him cry then." Then, on Tuesday, right after the accident, "There was a point in time when we were having breakfast where he'd break down and cry, and that was the first time I've ever seen him cry," said Sampson.

Allan Walker recalled that for weeks after the crash, any time Bergna came to visit he would sit in the Walkers' dining room and drift off.

"Peter, you OK?" they'd ask him.

He would take a deep breath, close his eyes and say, "Yeah, I'm OK."

He also continued to take the position that he had nothing to hide from authorities. Shortly after the crash, he complained to Mark James Jenness, a lawyer who lived across the street, that the police questioning had seemed to last too long and took too accusatory of a course.

"Peter, you better think about getting a lawyer here," Jenness told him.

"Well," Bergna replied, "I've got my dad. He is helping me. My dad is a lawyer."

Jenness suggested that perhaps Bergna should get a practicing criminal lawyer, not a retired prosecutor, but Bergna expressed surprise that this would be needed, saying, "What do I need a lawyer for?" Jenness shrugged, and the two talked about the usual topics of Incline Village life: the weather, the stock market, bears that wandered into the neighborhood from the woods. In short, Peter Bergna was acting like everything he was claiming to be: an innocent man tortured by his wife's violent death in a car crash that he might have been able to avoid. He remained on good terms with Rinette's family, even as they became more suspicious of him. The day after the crash, when Peter returned from his first police interview and was asked by Rinette's younger brother Richard about the circumstances of the accident, giving the story of the brakes that wouldn't brake and being thrown from the window, the two men were able to calmly discuss the arrangements for Rinette.

"Peter," Richard asked him, "what do you have in mind here as far as the services?"

"Oh, I haven't thought about it," Peter said.

"Do you have a Catholic cemetery in Incline?"

The neighbor, Mrs. Walker, who went to church with Rinette, told them that there was a Catholic cemetery in Reno.

"No," Rick said. "You're not gonna bury Rinette in

Christmas was Rinette Bergna's favorite holiday. Although she decided not to have children of her own, she lavished presents on her nieces and nephews. *Courtesy of Riella family.*

Peter Bergna. He and his wife, Rinette, lived in a comfortable chalet in Incline Village, an upscale resort community on the Nevada side of Lake Tahoe, in the mountains above Reno. Peter operated his antiques appraising business out of his home. *Courtesy of Riella family.*

The couple was married in 1987 when Peter was 35 years old and Rinette was 38. Peter was captivated by her vivacious personality; she loved his sophistication and gregariousness. The marriage would turn sour in a decade when Rinette wanted to give up her well-paying job as a pharmacist and travel the world as a lower-paid tour guide. Peter said he couldn't take the loneliness when she was away. *Both courtesy of Riella family.*

Shortly after Peter Bergna's Ford F-150 went over a cliff just after midnight on June 1, 1998, rescue workers used a safety rope to work their
way down to the wreckage, where they found Rinette, dead, dangling
from her seat belt. Her airbag had been turned off. Peter was found
hundreds of feet up the hill, just 80 feet down from the guardrail.
Courtesy of Washoe County District Attorney's Office.

A couple of days after the crash, the wreckage had to be flown out because the terrain was so rough and the hillside so steep. The truck was later inspected by a mechanic who found no evidence of brake or steering failure. Peter said he thought he was hitting the brakes but the truck wasn't stopping. *Courtesy of Washoe County District Attorney's Office.*

LEFT TOP: Peter's Ford F-150 pickup with a shell on the back crashed through a guardrail and tumbled down the steep mountainside, coming to a rest, upside down, 700 feet below in a bed of manzanita. Behind it was a trail of debris, including two plastic gas cans. The sealer caps were missing, and although gas was splattered everywhere, somehow the truck didn't explode on impact. *Courtesy of Washoe County District Attorney's Office.*

LEFT BOTTOM: The curve in the road, where Bergna's pickup went over the edge. Investigators felt that even if the brakes had failed, Peter could have easily turned into the hillside on the left and avoided the guardrail, yet they found no skid marks or evidence of leaking brake, transmission or steering fluid on the roadway. This area is used by hang glider enthusiasts—it's thousands of feet almost straight up from the valley floor. Peter had visited the site the day before the crash. *Courtesy of Washoe County District Attorney's Office.*

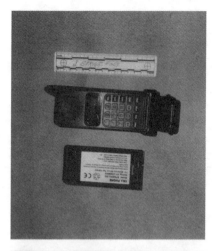

LEFT: The cell phone is the one Peter used to call 911 from the hillside. The emergency operator was surprised that Peter could have been thrown from the truck and still able to hold onto the phone, which was almost unscathed. Peter would say he didn't know how he got out of the truck or why he was so far up the hill while the wreckage was down lower. *Courtesy of Washoe County District Attorney's Office.*

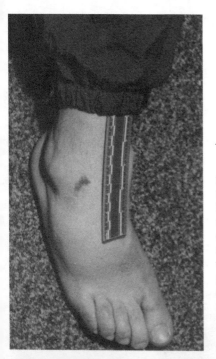

FACING PAGE AND THIS PAGE: These pictures of Peter with injuries were taken just hours after the crash at the sheriff's substation in Incline Village, where Peter lived. Investigators were immediately suspicious that Peter had not suffered more serious injuries. *All courtesy of Washoe County District Attorney's Office.*

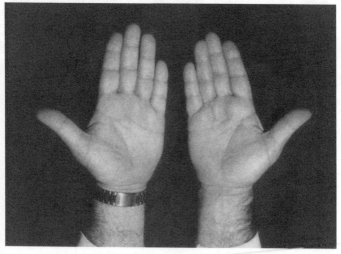

Young Rinette Riella.
Courtesy of Riella family.

The steep cliff where she died. *Courtesy of Washoe County District Attorney's Office.*

Reno. She liked Incline, I would go for that, but you're not going to bury her in Reno."

To Peter, he said, "Peter, look, why don't you let us bring Rinette home? We'll bury her next to Mom and Dad." Then he suggested that when Peter felt better they could have a memorial service in Incline.

Peter agreed: two services, one in Manteca, one in Incline.

But while the discussion ended in a compromise, it also signaled a growing rift between Peter and Rinette's family—two services and, soon, two camps.

It was a traditional Catholic funeral with a Mass. Rinette's casket sat in the church in Manteca, which was filled with friends and her large family. Peter wore sunglasses. Again, nobody saw a tear. But those who knew him said he was emotionally reeling. At one point, he went up to Rinette's casket and knelt. When he arose, he appeared to be in a daze.

Meanwhile, the growing divide between the Bergna and Riella families darkened an already somber ceremony. Some of Peter and Rinette's friends had grumbled that the main service was held in Manteca, on the other side of the Sierra Nevada, rather than in Incline where the couple lived and worked. In the church, Rinette's family sat in one area, Peter and his family and friends in another. "It was horrible," Adelaide Gramanz would later say. "I think he felt isolated." Peter's mother, Patricia Bergna, would later observe, "It just didn't seem like we were part of it somehow. It was more the Riellas were doing that part of it. I wouldn't say bad feelings. It just— Maybe cold, a little bit cold, but I could understand, too, in a way." After the service, as people were filing out of the church, Rinette's relatives were reluctant to embrace him.

"Peter," Rinette's brother Richard finally told him, "it would be better if you left now."

And so he did, with members of his family. That night, at the hotel, he wandered around the lawn and seemed to stare off into the distance. Relatives came down to fetch him, but, seeing him there, they let him be, and returned to their rooms.

Later, at the second service held for Rinette, this one a memorial at the Catholic church in Incline Village, with a reception afterwards at a country club, Peter was on his turf and "was a little more relaxed," said Gramanz, "because he was surrounded by friends." His mother said, "He was trying to greet people that came to honor Rinette. He was just doing the best he could to handle it."

But one guest, Rinette's former tour guide boss at Tauck Tours, Kendra St. John, found Peter's behavior at first odd—then disturbing. St. John had flown into Reno from Connecticut, her plane arriving late. She drove her rental car up to Incline—along Mount Rose Highway— and went to the church, arriving just as the service was finishing. She then went to the luncheon at the country club, where she saw Peter. "I gave him a hug and said I was very sorry," she recalled. "I felt familiar with him to some degree and I felt very bad for having lost his wife in this accident and I gave him a hug and expressed my condolences."

While at the lunch, St. John told Bergna that she had to send some urgent faxes—immigration materials—and asked if there was a fax machine in the area. He said he had one in the basement office at his house. He walked her out to her rental car, giving her directions to his house, and she noticed that he had a cast on his foot.

"Sorry about your foot," she told him. "How's it doing?"

"It's really not that bad," he said. "I wish I'd been hurt worse. I wish I'd broken my neck."

A strange feeling came over St. John. She thought it was unusual that he didn't say he wished he'd broken his neck if only it would have *saved* his wife. But that was only the first strange thing she encountered that afternoon. Bergna and other men at the luncheon were standing around smoking cigars, and, "It seemed very casual," recalled St. John. "There wasn't a lot of emotion or grief visible."

Bergna drove with her to the house. While there, he showed her some memorabilia from the World Cup—they'd had that soccer coach friend in common, as they'd discovered when they first met at a tour-guide function during Rinette's training—and then he came over to her, put his arm around her and said, "You know, any time you need a place to stay in Incline Village, come out and visit. Stay as long as you want. You're always welcome here. You've got a home here."

St. John suddenly felt very uncomfortable. She didn't know what Bergna was trying to do. He seemed too affectionate.

She would complete her faxing, then leave Incline Village for her drive back down the mountain for the airport. On the way down, she made a detour, turning right on the Slide Mountain access road and driving to the crash site. She had spoken to Bergna about the details of the accident, how he had taken Rinette up the hill after her return from Italy to look at the lights in the valley, and, "It seemed fishy to me and I wanted to see the site myself," she said. St. John knew that Rinette would have just ended a long, arduous flight after an extended stay in Italy for two training tours and her first solo tour. It would seem that Rinette would have been exhausted and in need of a good night's sleep rather than a trip to a romantic scenic overlook. At the crash site, St. John saw flowers on a shiny new section that had been put up to replace the mangled guardrail.

She got out of the car, walked to the railing and peered over the precipice. "I kept thinking of Rinette," she would later say, "and how horrible it must have been to go off the edge."

———

Chapter 20

Kendra St. John would be among the first people interviewed by the Washoe County Sheriff's Office as part of what would become a lengthy and sporadic investigation, the department again seeing no benefit in haste. It was starting to appear that there would be no single piece of evidence, no smoking gun, that would crack the case, but that a large mosaic of evidence would have to be collected and assembled. As such, Detective James Beltron and later Detective Larry Canfield, who would take over for Beltron, wanted to dissect Bergna's long statements in the interviews to draw a full picture of his life with Rinette, to see what was true, what wasn't, and what could be used against him in court, if it came to that. Bergna had made so much of his wife's new career as a tour guide, and the pain it caused him for her to be away, that the investigators knew this was a critical area, perhaps pointing to a motive, and they wanted to talk to St. John and others about Rinette's career change.

What they found was that nearly everything that Peter

said was true. For their entire marriage, Rinette loved to travel, and by all accounts Peter seemed to share in this passion. But when Rinette became a tour guide, leaving Peter behind, everything changed. Investigators found that Peter's complaints of loneliness were not exaggerated. Friends and Rinette's family told story after story of how much Peter hated having Rinette away from home.

But the most compelling evidence was contained in Peter's own pocket. As investigators went through the clothing that Bergna had worn the night of the crash, they uncovered a document written the night that Rinette had telefaxed "Peterski" from Italy saying that she would see him the following Sunday.

Written on a computer and filled with grammatical errors and misspellings, it read:

Agreement to improve our marriage
5.26.98

Peter   Rinette

1. Improve our self love
2. Love the other person
3. Listen to the other persons ideas
4. Compermise with our ideas
5. Impelment our ideas
6. Work for common goals
7. Be kind to others
8. Take control of our money & bills
9. Deal with problems as they arise
10. Use common sense when dealing with problems.
11. Make love more often

Chapter 21

Police found that the night after drafting this agreement a moody Peter Bergna attended a retirement party for an old friend, Incline High School Principal Mike Whellams, where Peter told anybody who would listen how much he missed his wife. Karen Owen, an elementary school teacher who lived across the street from the Bergnas, spent much of the evening at the crowded party for the popular principal with two old friends, Maxine Preston and Joan Dunklee, who were tending bar. At one point, Bergna, whom she knew more as an acquaintance than as a close friend, sidled up to the bar and in a strange, disjointed and sad way blurted out, "Well, as you know, my wife's gone again."

At first the women thought he had been drinking, but they smelled no alcohol on his breath.

"No," said Owen, trying to figure out a nice thing to say, "I didn't realize this."

Dunklee, who also knew the Bergnas, though not well,

recalled that Peter then started telling the women how all he really wanted in life was a wife who would stay home and give him children. Why, Dunklee wondered, was he telling her this?

Chapter 22

Peter Bergna had always made it clear that he wanted children. He came from a family of four children, he spent much of his free time coaching youth soccer, and he adored the Walker brood, helping them with their sports and taking them on excursions, like the trip to the side of Slide Mountain the day before the accident. But there was a problem. As he told investigators in his interview, "I've wanted children all my life and so forth and she [Rinette] does not." He had acknowledged, "that was a real kind of bone of contention for me. I really wanted children . . ."

Peter's friend Mark Steven Sampson would recall, "I know Peter had discussions on occasion with both my wife and I that there was desire on his part to have children." But Peter would say that as the years passed, he realized it was unsafe for Rinette to be pregnant. "They considered adoption, since he was adopted," recalled Sampson. "I do know that Rinette did not want to have children, and that was a topic of conversation for them . . . I'm really not sure as to whether it was because he truly wanted children or if he wanted to be around people. . . . It was an issue, but I don't think it was one where they were butting heads." Clearly, however, the absence of children in the Bergna chalet only increased the loneliness.

The revelations about Peter hating it when Rinette was away and he was having to stay home in a quiet childless house clearly showed to investigators rifts in the marriage leading up to the moment that the truck went off the cliff. It could be seen as, if not *the* murder motive, a contributing factor: She wouldn't grant him his desire to stay home more, so out of hurt and anger he killed her. But at the same time, it could support Peter's own logic that there was no reason to kill his wife out of loneliness. Eliminating her would only make him more—and permanently—lonely.

But as the investigation ground on, detectives found signs that Peter may not have been as lonely as he suggested—and that he looked to more than the TV set for companionship. The first clue came from a man named Leo J. Humphreys, who, as vice president and trust administrator for the Wells Fargo Bank in Reno, worked with a number of appraisers, including Bergna. Humphreys would tell investigators that in the first or second week of May, while Bergna's wife was in Europe on her training tours for Tauck, Bergna spoke to Humphreys about another employee of Wells Fargo—a woman named Janet Mello, a senior credit officer in the private banking division. Bergna asked Humphreys if she happened to be married or seeing anybody. Complaining that he didn't want to sit at home alone while his wife was away, Bergna told Humphreys he might want to ask Mello out to the movies. Humphreys politely said he didn't want to have anything to do with this and that if Bergna wanted to ask Janet out, he would have to do it himself.

Investigators also found out that on the night before Rinette's return, on Saturday, May 30, 1998, Bergna attended a second party in addition to the retirement event that week in Incline Village, this one a surprise 40th birthday bash at the Hacienda De La Sierra, a popular Mexican restaurant for locals, for a friend named Teresa Flores. An employee with the Southwest Gas Corporation, Teresa had known Bergna for about five years. They met at Incline Village Middle School when Bergna was helping coach her daughter's American Youth Soccer Organization team. They had been platonic friends, meeting for lunch or dinner on occasion. Bergna arrived at the party early, around 5 p.m., to join the others in awaiting Flores, and as they stood around, Bergna met another woman, Brenda Redl-Harge, who, like Janet Mello, was an attractive blonde. They made small talk, with Bergna asking Brenda if she was married or had any children. She told him she wasn't married, but had two daughters. Brenda then left to pick up the birthday girl, and while she was away, Bergna started talking to Brenda's friend, Audrey Tedore, who at the time worked at the same Wells Fargo Bank as Leo Humphreys and Janet Mello. "He was telling me about this art collection that he had because of his business, that he appraised art, so he had a big art collection and everyone there was telling me how fabulous it was," recalled Audrey. "So he invited me to come see it."

It was going to be a while before Teresa showed up, and Bergna's house was close by, so Audrey got into Bergna's blue Ford F-150 pickup and the two went to his house, where they stayed for about forty-five minutes. He showed her his artwork in the living room, then took her downstairs to his office area where there was more art and some wines, before they returned to the Hacienda. Audrey recalled that he was "very nice, very polite, very courteous"—to a point. "Towards the end of leaving, I just, you know, I felt like he was pretty close," she recalled. "He maybe stood a little closer, looked me in the eye a little too long, but other than that, that was maybe it. . . . It just made me feel uncomfortable because, I don't know, I just felt like he was too interested in me."

Bergna brought Audrey back to the Hacienda at about 8:15 p.m. for the surprise party, which went well into the evening and would continue, late, at another location, a dance club called Legends. The heartiest of the birthday partiers, including Bergna, drove to the club, where the group took to the dance floor, except Bergna, who was in a patio area. "He motioned for me to come out, and he was sitting on a bench," she said, "and I just walked up to him, and he said, 'Would you go out to dinner with me?' and I told him, 'No,' that I would not, 'because you're married.' He just kind of shrugged his shoulders and kind of looked down and I turned around and went back in and joined the rest of the people dancing."

Bergna didn't give up. He tried to dance only with Audrey, but she just wanted to dance with the group. She asked her friend Brenda to "run interference" with Bergna to keep him away from her, which Brenda said she did. At some point Bergna left the club, alone.

As investigators reviewed these details from Leo Humphreys, Audrey Tedore and Brenda Redl-Harge, it seemed to contradict what Peter Bergna had said during his post-crash interview: "I don't go out. I don't go hit the bars. I'm not out looking for women. I stay home. And that gets someone like myself lonely." At another point in the interviews, he'd said: "I'm not out trying to meet other women and so forth." Yet now investigators had witnesses saying he *was* trying to meet other women. As Detective Larry Canfield, who interviewed the women, recalled, "We didn't have a sexual encounter, but we had the next best thing."

What's more, after the death of Rinette, Bergna wasted very little time in reestablishing contact with these women. Three to four weeks after the accident, Bergna called Janet Mello. Bergna and Janet had actually met a couple of times professionally. Bergna did appraisal work for many of Wells Fargo's elderly trust clients, and Janet had seen him about two months before the accident at the Old Town Mall in Reno at an appraisal fair, where people would bring in jewelry and artwork and other items for Bergna to look over on behalf of Butterfields. Janet didn't work in the trust section, but because the woman who did couldn't make it to the fair, she went in her place. Janet hadn't spoken to Bergna since the fair, until one day, in June 1998, she got a call from him at her office.

"This is Peter Bergna," he said. It was Wednesday or Thursday. "I apologize for calling you at work for a personal matter, but I didn't have your home phone."

Her number was unlisted. He asked her if she would be interested in going out to a movie with him on Friday night. Finding the whole thing strange—she had heard about Bergna's wife's death in the accident—Janet turned him down.

This didn't seem to discourage Bergna. Around the same time, he reintroduced himself to Brenda Redl-Harge, the woman he met at the party for Teresa Flores. Using crutches, Bergna limped into Brenda's office at the bank and talked to her about the accident, saying that the brakes had given out and that he had flown through the window. He never said anything about missing his dead wife or expressed any grief over her demise. He did complain that police had spent long hours with him and that he was frustrated.

Bergna would see Brenda several times again in the month after the accident, either at her office or at their mutual friend Teresa Flores' house while Brenda was also visiting. "He called me at least once a week," recalled Brenda. "[He] wanted me to see his art collection. When was I gonna be up at the lake again? I guess I didn't take it seriously. I figured he knew Teresa, and I was a friend of Teresa's. I was just kind of 'OK, yeah, whatever, I'll be there.' Sometime, you know, but more 'I'll be with Teresa' or 'I'm gonna meet Teresa up there.' 'Teresa and I are going to do something, I'll talk to her'–type deal."

They also spent time together at a Fourth of July beach party on the shores of Lake Tahoe. It was the Optimist Club's annual fund-raising picnic, and Bergna helped babysit Brenda's 4-year-old daughter Laura while Brenda and her friends Audrey and Teresa sold tickets to the party. Brenda was impressed with how well Bergna got along with little Laura. Bergna would tell Brenda that he had always wanted to have children of his own but that his late wife didn't want to.

Bergna was quickly becoming something of a local player, and his time with Brenda caused ripples with Teresa, who had known Bergna long before Brenda came on the scene. Teresa would complain that it was Brenda trying to put the moves on Peter, and that the day of the Fourth of July party, her behavior was inappropriate, essentially abandoning her daughter with Bergna so that she could go out boating. At one point, Brenda even dropped her top while on the boat, Teresa would complain. "Brenda would say, 'Peter likes you,' " recalled Teresa. "My take on it was Brenda was trying to find out my feelings—if I had any—for Peter, to see if she had an OK, the green light to be his friend more so than what I was."

In any event, Bergna would open up with Brenda as they continued to see each other for picnics or a lunch at Togos restaurant with her daughter. He would continue to talk about the accident, telling her that he and his wife had gone up to Slide Mountain to resolve some issues about her long absences for the tour guide job. He told her that he had asked his wife for a divorce several times, but she didn't want to go through with it because she didn't want to admit that she had failed at something. He complained about money, about how he was going to continue making payments on Rinette's Chevy Blazer now that he was living on one income and facing possible cash problems. And he complained about how long police were taking to wrap up the investigation and clear him.

In the second week of July, six weeks after the accident, Bergna asked Brenda if she and her daughter would like to come over to his house for dinner, take a look at his art collection and soak in his hot tub. Brenda agreed.

The evening started out well enough. Bergna grilled them steaks on the barbecue and opened a bottle of wine. But then, after dinner, Laura went into the living room to watch some videos she had brought. As Bergna turned on the television, the Playboy Channel appeared on the screen.

Brenda looked at Bergna, and he just said, "Well, I have needs, too."

Brenda's daughter would fall asleep on the sofa watching the videos. As she slept, Brenda and Bergna got into his hot tub in the back yard. Brenda says they sat well apart from each other and both were wearing swimsuits. At one point, Bergna asked her to move closer to him and said, "Oh, you could see the stars better over here."

"I'm fine," she said, nervously.

Bergna then moved over to her side. She moved to her left, away from him. But he got closer anyway. He put his arm around her shoulder and then touched her breast.

She abruptly told him to stop. Bergna got mad and asked what was wrong. Brenda told him she wanted to go home. She scooped up Laura and headed for the door.

Before she left, Bergna offered her a gift: Rinette's golf club set. Bergna knew that Brenda's older daughter Mallory, then 10 years old, was learning to play golf, and that the girl was about the same height as Rinette.

"Shouldn't these go to the family?" Brenda asked. She felt awkward taking them.

But Bergna put the clubs in the trunk of her car, saying he wanted to start getting rid of Rinette's things. "You might as well use them if your daughter's learning how to golf," he said.

The night in the hot tub would be as far as Bergna ever got with Brenda romantically. A few days later he showed up at her office and gave her a Hallmark card as an apology and offered to take her out to lunch. She accepted, and they went to the Wine and Cheeseboard in Reno in the third week of July. During the lunch he was polite, businesslike, and tried no more moves on her. They agreed to remain friends.

Chapter 23

As the summer of 1998 turned to fall and then winter, and the snows came to the mountains, Peter Bergna began to feel a chill of a much different sort. There were the nasty looks he got in the street, the eyes that would be averted when he walked into a favorite restaurant. Longtime friends from his volunteer activities stopped calling him. "He was angry at how some people had been treating him in Incline, how some people had abandoned him, and I felt he was very disappointed with that," recalled his friend Mark Steven Sampson. "But mostly what I felt from him was, you know, just loneliness and slight depression. I wouldn't say it's deep depression, but slight depression."

The frostiest of relations was between Peter and Rinette's family. From the very beginning they had been skeptical of his story of the brakes that wouldn't brake, of being thrown out of a window, and of being unable to remember critical moments of the crash. Suddenly, every irritating thing that Bergna had done over the past fourteen years seemed to take on a new, more sinister meaning. They thought of Bergna's flashes of temper, how he had once stomped away at an airport customs counter in Chicago because Rinette had had the audacity to hyphenate her last name as Riella-Bergna rather than just use his surname. They thought of the time during a trip to Italy when Bergna had blown up because she had borrowed $20 from her brother to buy a souvenir. When she asked Bergna to pay back her brother, he'd fumed, "You keep your own finances. That's your money, not mine, and I keep everything separate." They thought of the time that Bergna had used the F-word in front of the Riella children at a Christmas Eve dinner just because he didn't like the pasta. They told themselves that they'd always found him a little condescending toward Rinette and the rest of her farm-raised family. Bergna would always talk a little too loudly, stand a little too closely, crave just a little too much attention. Whether this was a reaction to growing up with a prominent man like Lou Bergna or whether he was just a bit of an arrogant pill would never be clear. All they knew was that after Rinette died, and Bergna's stories didn't add up, the Riella family's animosity toward him grew.

Bergna did nothing in the months after the crash to endear himself to them. The tensions that surfaced at the funeral only increased as the months went past. Richard Riella recalled that after the funeral he drove to Incline Village to retrieve some of the family belongings that Rinette had taken when their mother died. When Richard arrived at the house about a month after the accident, he was shocked to find hardly any evidence that his sister had ever lived there. Rinette's clothes were gone, her pharmaceutical awards were packed away and all the pictures of Riella family members were taken off the counters and the walls. They asked about Rinette's wedding dress; that was gone too. Bergna was even planning on selling their wedding china at a Butterfields auction.

About three months after the accident, on Richard Riella's third and final trip to Incline Village to get family belongings, he sat down with Bergna and again went over the crash. When he'd talked to him the morning after the accident, Bergna had said the brakes didn't work. By that last visit, Bergna was now saying that maybe he had the sensation of the brakes not working and that he may have actually been hitting the accelerator. Richard asked him why he had newly filled gas cans in the back of the pickup. First Bergna had said he needed the extra gas for a trip to Las Vegas. Then he said he'd needed the gas for his snow blower. Richard and his brothers were now not convinced that their sister had died in an accident. And if it wasn't an accident, they felt that Bergna should not get a penny of her family inheritance.

About six to eight months after the crash, the brothers told Bergna that since, in Richard's words, "Things weren't too kosher here," they were going to try to block Bergna from getting his cut of the $664,000 in farm property. Bergna hired an attorney to fight for his share. The brothers met with their attorneys. Soon, they were communicating only through counsel and the tone was nasty. Both sides were on the brink of an all-out legal battle when Richard suggested, during a meeting with his brothers and their lawyers, "Why don't you let me try to call him and see what I can do?"

Richard made the call to his former brother-in-law.

"Peter," Richard said, "we need to talk and get this resolved."

"No, Rick, I don't think so," Bergna said, according to Richard.

"Why?" asked Richard.

"Well, you guys tried to screw me and you tried to put this money in an account so I couldn't get it." Bergna told him that not only was he entitled to the one-third share of the property, but that his share should be more than the $220,000 that the brothers had estimated it to be. Bergna felt that the farm property had been undervalued at $664,000.

He felt his share should be $400,000.

"Look, Peter," Richard said, getting angry. "Peter, our family has been here for three generations. We worked on this ranch. Just because you were married to my sister ten years and lived up here in Tahoe doesn't give you the right to get $400,000 out of this."

"I can't believe you said that, Rick," said Bergna, according to Richard. "I need to get all the money I can. I lost the earning potential of your sister for the next thirteen to fifteen years."

Richard was stunned. He felt that the man responsible for killing his sister was now talking only about her lost earning potential.

Richard told him that in the Riella family's opinion, anything Peter Bergna got was a gift. But, finally, Richard suggested a compromise: the family would give Bergna a cut—not the $400,000 he wanted, but the $220,000 that the Riellas had originally claimed the share was worth.

"Peter, at this point, we're willing to just give you the money," Richard said. "We'll meet at Roseville or Sacramento, halfway point. We'll go to a notary, I'll bring you a check for $220,000, we'll call this even."

In the end, they settled on a $275,000 cash payout to Bergna. The brothers didn't like it, but they felt it was the best they were going to do without spending the rest of their money on lawyers' fees.

• • •

But even as Bergna was fighting the Riella brothers, he wasn't starved for cash. On April 30, 1999, while he was seeking a cut of the Riella farmland inheritance, a check from the Safeco Insurance Company arrived in the amount of $472,596.07. The money included the $450,000 policy payout plus interest. Bergna's insurance broker, Ronald Wright, personally delivered the check to Bergna's house. "Peter was surprised," Wright recalled. "He was not aware that it would be that large a check. He seemed to have forgotten about the $200,000 accidental death."

Neighbors soon noticed that Bergna had been making some big-ticket purchases: a new boat, new cars. He would take vacations to London, Hawaii, Mexico and Canada. By May 1999, one year after the crash, with Bergna still a free man and spending lots of what the Riella family considered to be blood money, Rinette's brothers went to court, filing a wrongful death suit against him. Seeking punitive and other damages, the lawsuit claimed that Bergna "intentionally and deliberately caused the vehicle to leave the road and off the mountainside for the purpose of causing injury and/or death to his wife" and that he was the "culpable" person for the "felonious and intentional death" of Rinette Riella-Bergna. The Riella brothers said money wasn't the motivation for the lawsuit. "We wanted him under oath to tell what happened to our sister on that hill," said Richard. "He told me three different stories. All we wanted was the truth."

The search for the truth was a slow and deliberate one. Weeks turned to months, and months turned to a year, then another year, and still the sheriff's department didn't have enough evidence to arrest Peter Bergna. The snail's pace of the investigation would be attributed to a number of factors, not the least of which was that many people inside both the sheriff's department and the DA's office didn't think there was sufficient evidence to prove that Bergna had committed murder. The opinions stretched from the notion that it looked like an accident to the belief that it probably was a murder, but that there wasn't proof of guilt beyond a reasonable doubt.

The Peter Bergna investigation went back and forth from the back burner to the front. Detectives went about interviewing witnesses with details about Bergna's amorous activities before and after the crash. They talked to Richard Riella and other members of Rinette's family to find out about the inheritance and Bergna's temper flashes in the past. They spoke to the insurance people to see how much money Bergna was getting. In September 1999, Trooper John Schilling and others got a Ford truck similar to the one Bergna drove and trekked up to the mountain to conduct a semi-reenactment of the crash. They didn't drive the truck off the cliff, but they did drive it around the bend at several different speeds—at one point they even gunned it to 50 mph—and each time they were able to easily make the broad left turn on the banking roadway without risk of going into the guardrail. The reenactment was videotaped in case it would ever be needed in court.

Each new piece of evidence was interesting enough, building toward what someday might be a good enough circumstantial case to present to a jury. But as the months went by, that day had yet to arrive. One big reason for the stalled investigation was the large number of questions surrounding the truck's airbag. From the very beginning, the explanation of when Bergna's airbag had inflated—and where he was at the time—could make or break the case. At first, Beltron had thought he had Bergna because there was no apparent dust on his clothing from the cornstarch used as a lubricant for the airbag. That would mean that Bergna was out of the truck at the time the airbag inflated, probably when it hit the guardrail, strongly suggesting he had staged the accident. But if there was any airbag residue on his clothing, then that meant he had been *in* the truck when it inflated at the guardrail and could have been thrown out the window as it went down the hill, as he'd claimed. The scenario still struck investigators as far-fetched, but cornstarch on the clothes could be exploited by a good defense attorney to prove reasonable doubt.

To resolve this, Bergna's jacket and other clothes were sent to the Washoe County sheriff's crime lab for inspection under a microscope, and the lab found signs of cornstarch on the jacket. Not a lot, but it was clearly there. Since Rinette's airbag had been shut off, it had to have come from Bergna's airbag, meaning there was evidence, albeit microscopically small, that Bergna was in the truck when it hit the guardrail and could have been thrown out.

Investigators also went to Ford, who, in the months after the crash, had submitted a report that said this particular airbag, manufactured by TRW, didn't use cornstarch as a lubricant, but another material. That would mean there was *no* cornstarch from the airbag, and instead the cornstarch on Bergna's clothes must have come from other sources. It turned out that the gloves worn by the rescue people who'd handled Bergna were also lubricated with cornstarch. Also, there was evidence that cornstarch is simply a naturally occurring material flying all over the place in the air. But the next report from Ford, in 1999, contradicted the first one: Yes, there was cornstarch used as a lubricant, but not very much of it. The bag wasn't lubricated with cornstarch, but the little heat shield over it was. That meant that a very small amount of cornstarch could have gotten on Bergna's clothing from the airbag exploding at the guardrail.

Then investigators considered yet another aspect to the airbag issue. Until now, they had assumed it inflated when the truck hit the guardrail. What if the airbag *didn't* deploy at the guardrail, but later, when the truck hit the side of the mountain, long after Bergna had left the vehicle under any scenario?

The original report from Ford had said that the bag probably would have inflated when the truck smashed into the guardrail. But when investigators had looked at the guardrail, they found that it was not as formidable a barrier as might be expected. It was supposed to be held to the wooden post by five bolts, but on the night of the accident, four bolts were missing. Only one bolt had held the two thirteen-foot-long metal rail sections to the post. Although they were suspicious of Bergna, detectives didn't go so far as to think he had been the one to remove the bolts. Hang glider enthusiasts had told investigators that they had heard the bolts were removed years earlier to provide more room for a hang-gliding event. Also, there appeared to be rust around the bolt holes, suggesting they had been missing for some time. That wasn't to say, however, that investigators didn't suspect Bergna knew the bolts were missing. He had been up there just the day before the crash.

The missing bolts would have presumably weakened the guardrail, providing so little resistance that not only did the truck smash through, but it did so without enough of a jolt to trigger the airbag. To see if this happened, Highway Patrol investigators including Detective Larry Canfield, along with a Ford scientist and representatives from Bergna's insurance company, went up to the mountain in June 2000 to test the strength of the guardrail, or, more specifically, the wooden four-inch-by-four-inch post that held up the metal railings. They wanted to know how much force it would take to knock over the post. A tremendous amount of force would mean that the truck's speed would slow dramatically and quickly, triggering the airbag. But a smaller amount of force would show that the truck sailed through the barely-bolted guardrail and off the cliff, with the airbag not opening until the vehicle smashed into the ground. At the crash site, technicians hooked up cables to a guardrail post, fastened the other end to a pine tree, then slowly tightened the wire to see how much force was needed to yank the post from the ground. Canfield said the post came out "with very little force." That proved to investigators that the airbag didn't open at the guardrail. No matter when Bergna had left the truck—just before or just after crashing through the guardrail—the airbag wouldn't have yet opened, and it wouldn't have left any dust on him.

The test not only laid to rest, in investigators' minds anyway, the airbag dust issue, but it provided them with another piece of information. Because the post yielded with so little force, that was evidence the truck may not have been going as fast as everyone assumed. From the very beginning, Detective Beltron and others believed that the truck had to have been barreling toward the guardrail at 40 mph or more to build up enough force to crash through. That would have set up the daredevil maneuver by Bergna if he had jumped out of the racing truck before the impact. It also would have meant, as Bergna himself pointed out during the interview, that if he had bailed out onto asphalt at 40 mph, he should have suffered more serious injury. But the test showing the weakness of the guardrail post now suggested that the truck could have been going much slower to get through the railing, maybe less than 20 mph.

That would have made Bergna's jump less treacherous—and his injuries more in line with what he really had: a few scrapes and a twisted ankle.

There would be a delicious irony for investigators. In reviewing the notes of Bergna's interview they would find that Bergna himself insisted that he was going about 20 mph.

Chapter 24

At various stages as the investigation inched along, Detectives Beltron and Canfield had wanted to speak with Bergna again to go over the various developments, from the indication that Tauck Tours' Kendra St. John had given that Rinette was planning to spend even more time away, to the results of the tests on the airbag and the guardrail post. They were also interested in discussing the fact that an examination of the truck found no signs of brake failure. And they thought they might ask him about some of his lady friends. But Bergna, so cooperative in the days after the investigation—telling people he had nothing to hide and no need to hire a lawyer—had become scarce. Investigators knew where he lived and people saw him around town, so there were no fears that he would try to run away. But at the same time, he wasn't returning calls from Detective Canfield. When the detective would stop by the house in Incline, Bergna wouldn't be there, so he'd leave a business card. In time, Bergna would hire a criminal attorney, a local lawyer named

Frederick Pinkerton, and Canfield would try to contact Bergna through him. Again, no luck. Once, Bergna himself contacted the local sheriff, not to tell his side of the story again, but to report a burglary on his house. A gun had been stolen.

In the late spring or early summer of 1999, Peter Bergna was no longer in Incline Village. Canfield had received word that Bergna had moved to Washington state and was continuing to work for Butterfields out of his home in Seattle.

Canfield also got word that there was a new woman in Bergna's life.

It was five months after the crash, in the fall of 1998, that Bergna had met Robin Russell, a trust officer for a Seattle bank. Robin had just turned 40 and Peter, she would later say, was still mourning the loss of his wife. "We both just needed a friend," she would tell the *Reno Gazette-Journal*. Bergna's employee, Adelaide Gramanz, confirmed that Bergna was an emotional wreck at the time. He couldn't work, so she picked up the appraisals. He would watch TV, go to lunch by himself, and mope. Gramanz said that Butterfields officials knew that she was doing most of the work, and they wanted Bergna to get out of the house and become sociable again. So the company sent Bergna on a fly-fishing trip with several Butterfields clients to the Trinity Alps in Northern California, where he met Robin. "Robin really was pressuring him," Gramanz would later tell a jury. "She really wanted to have a commitment from him. I think she really wanted to get married. She's always been single and here she meets a guy she really likes. I think she was putting too much pressure on him. He wasn't ready at all. He really wasn't over Rinette."

Still, Gramanz had to acknowledge that it was a new Bergna who returned to Incline, more focused on his work, more energetic. He kept in touch with Robin, who returned to Seattle, and he confided to Gramanz that "he hadn't met anyone nearly as wonderful as her," Gramanz said. During a vacation to Hawaii, Bergna proposed to Russell. They set a February 1999 wedding date, but they broke up, then reconciled. Bergna asked Butterfields if he could move his operations to the Northwest—where Robin lived, and in a market in which Butterfields was already interested. The company approved of the move. Bergna kept his home and office in Incline, where Gramanz would stay, and in May or June of 1999 he went to Seattle, where he and Robin made nice life for themselves. Through it all, Robin never believed that Bergna had killed Rinette. "Every time I was with him at one of these [business] functions, or when I would talk to him on the phone, there were always these wonderful, loving people around," she would tell the *San Jose Mercury News*. "I don't think mean people attract nice people."

Although they still planned to get married, they didn't set a new date. Some complications in Bergna's life were on the horizon that would prevent any long-term planning.

The lengthy investigation into the 1998 truck crash was at last winding down. The Washoe County District Attorney's Office had reviewed the evidence and made a decision. The case was headed for a grand jury.

The DA wanted Peter Bergna tried on murder charges.

Chapter 25

Every so often in a criminal investigation there's one of those happy accidents, when hard work and skill have to take a back seat to the whims of chance. Just such a moment occurred in the fall of 2000, as Chief Deputy District Attorney Dave Clifton and Sheriff's Detective Larry Canfield, the lead investigator on the case, were rummaging through the evidence room at sheriff's headquarters, going through the boxes and bags of materials collected in the Peter Bergna case. Clifton was a veteran supervisor in the DA's office—he had started in 1986—and was now overseeing a staff of seven deputies. He would cherry-pick the more difficult or high-profile cases for himself. This was just such a case.

Much of the evidence had long since been examined, and had sat in the evidence room for two years awaiting the day when—or if—the case would go to trial. As they went through the bags so Clifton could prepare for the grand jury, they came across the bag that contained Bergna's clothing—that same bag that had been picked up by sheriff's evidence man Jay Straits at Bergna's house the day the four officers escorted him to the substation for questioning. The clothes had already been examined by the sheriff's lab for traces of airbag dust. But apparently nobody had ever taken a good look at Bergna's tennis shoes.

"Oh, my God," Clifton said. "That's asphalt."

One of the shoes had brownish-black smudges. It would still need to be examined to be sure, but those smudges appeared to be road asphalt. If true, that would be powerful evidence that Bergna had gotten out of the truck on the turnout *before* it hit the guardrail, scuffing his shoes on the pavement after he leaped out.

This wouldn't be the only surprise. They looked at the two gas cans that Bergna had been carrying in the back of the truck—the cans that Bergna said he had filled up the night of the crash to use for his trip to Las Vegas, and to refuel his snow blower and other machines. They unscrewed the caps and found that something was missing. Canfield knew from experience with gas cans that inside the cap there should have been a little round plastic disk. The cap had a hole in it to make way for the nozzle, and the disk would be inserted to seal that hole. Yet the disks on both caps were gone. That meant that the cans were, for all intents and purposes, unsealed. Gas fumes would have filled the back of the truck, and if the cans had been knocked over, gas would have spilled everywhere. A small spark and everything would go up in flames. Bergna's explanation for the gas cans never struck Clifton as plausible to begin with. Now, it seemed preposterous. Clifton would review the transcript of Bergna's interview and one quote stood out: "When I finally figured out where I was, it was on the sand, I was sliding down the hill," Bergna had said. "I'm trying to the best I could, looked up and see if I could see the truck, see a fire . . ."

Chapter 26

Like most prosecutors in the West, David Clifton had heard of Lou Bergna—and of the Lou Bergna legend. Santa Clara County is not far from where Clifton had studied law, at McGeorge School of Law in Sacramento. He knew that Lou Bergna had been president of the same DA's organization of which Clifton was a member.

Clifton also knew that Lou Bergna was the father of the man he wanted nailed for murder. He had read the police reports and reviewed the transcripts of Peter Bergna's interviews in which he mentioned something about his father being the DA for Santa Clara County. And Clifton knew from the interview videotape that Lou Bergna had sat in on the final interview session, but didn't say much except to implore his son to tell the truth and to banter with James Beltron.

But what would come as a surprise to Clifton was that Lou Bergna, on the eve of the case going before the grand jury, wanted to talk to him. In private.

The request came personally from Lou Bergna in a

call to Clifton's office. Bergna was told that somebody would get back to him. It's not uncommon for a prosecutor to speak regularly with a defendant's attorney to handle evidence sharing, schedule court dates and go over other logistical matters. It also isn't unusual to hear from a defendant's family member. In Clifton's case it was usually an aggrieved mother pleading for her son's mercy.

But Lou Bergna was a little of both—a parent who also was an attorney. Clifton wondered what it was that Lou Bergna wanted. A sneak peek at the prosecution's evidence? Maybe make an attempt to block the case from ever going to a grand jury? Would Lou Bergna try to intimidate Clifton by dropping powerful names and throwing around a little bit of that political muscle he had built in the Santa Clara County DA's Office? Or might he try to sweet-talk Clifton, prosecutor to prosecutor?

Clifton and his boss, elected District Attorney Dick Gammick, decided they would meet with Lou Bergna. They also decided on a strategy for that meeting: all take and no give. They weren't going to be bullied by the former president of the National District Attorneys Association.

Louis Bergna came into the Washoe County DA's Office by himself. It was October of 2000, as best Clifton could remember. The long-since-retired prosecutor wore a suit and looked like he was ready to go to court. Clifton noticed Bergna's limp from the polio. The men exchanged greetings, and Bergna apologized for the problems with his right arm. He shook Clifton's right hand with his left. They then took their seats around a conference table.

Lou Bergna began by explaining that he believed in his son's innocence, which came as little surprise to Clifton and Gammick. He told them that Peter was adopted, like all his children, but that he and his wife loved him as if he were a natural-born son.

Then Bergna explained that he, too, had once been a prosecutor, working his entire professional life for Santa Clara County. He told them some folksy golf stories, and anecdotes from the old days in the office. But through it all he emphasized that he was pro–law enforcement to the bone. Speaking now lawyer-to-lawyer, Bergna told them that he knew that Clifton and Gammick had a job to do and that he knew, as a prosecutor, that no ethical DA would bring a murder case against a man unless he felt that he had the evidence. Bergna said he was confident that Clifton and Gammick truly believed they had that evidence. He told them that it was his idea that Bergna talk to the police, and he had urged his son to tell them everything he knew, to tell the truth. Bergna told them that he was not there to find out what their evidence was or to argue the case. And he said that while he supported Peter, if the evidence pointed to his son's guilt, Lou Bergna would no longer back him.

Clifton and Gammick were momentarily stunned. They found themselves addressing this man—the father of the man they were about to try to put away for life—as "Lou," instead of "Mr. Bergna." He was charming, modest, sincere and full of integrity; he was everything that everybody said and would say about him. Clifton also felt that there was a hint of apology in Bergna's voice—and perhaps regret. By the end of the one-hour meeting, Clifton felt that he could trust Lou Bergna.

"Lou," said Clifton, "I'm not going to talk to you about all the evidence. I will tell you that, yes, in my opinion there's enough to convict."

Clifton told Bergna that he planned to put about 75 percent of his case before the grand jury. The grand jury proceeding would only take a day or two—while the trial could last for weeks—but the biggest, most important pieces of the puzzle would be shown.

"You know and I know that when it goes to a jury we don't know what they'll do," said Clifton. "But I can tell you I have a firm belief that he's guilty."

"I respect you for talking to me, and I respect your decision," said Lou Bergna. "I want you to know that I still believe in his innocence. I don't know all the facts, and I don't know all the evidence. I know you have a job to do, and I want you to know that there's no animosity, because I sat in your seat."

And with that, Lou Bergna left.

Chapter 27

On November 15, 2000, the people of the state of Nevada presented their case against Peter Bergna to a grand jury. The heart of the prosecution's case—the 75 percent of it that Clifton had told Peter's father about—would include fifteen witnesses. It began with Trooper Rick McLellan testifying about the night he found Bergna with a cell phone, but no obvious injuries, lying on the hill, and ended with Richard Riella's bitter testimony about his tangles with Bergna over Rinette's inheritance. "We didn't want him to benefit from the death of my sister," said Richard. Also testifying were the highway patrol auto shop man, Dewey Dean Willie, who'd inspected the truck and found no brake problems; Dr. Roger Ritzlin, the pathologist who couldn't say whether Rinette was dead before the accident; Detective James Beltron to talk about the interviews with Bergna; Wells Fargo banker Janet Mello to talk about how Bergna had asked her out to a movie; the women at the principal's retirement party to testify about how Bergna was morose and missed his wife while she was in Italy; and witnesses to discuss the $450,000 in insurance money that Bergna received. Clifton also played a portion of the 911 tape.

But the most important part of the prosecution presentation was the testimony of Trooper John Schilling, who spoke to the grand jury not only as a witness on the scene but also as an expert accident reconstructionist, sharing his opinions about what he felt had really happened on the mountain. He told the grand jury that from the moment he saw Bergna on the side of the mountain, he was suspicious. "He didn't look like somebody who had been ejected from the vehicle and rolled down the hill," said Schilling. "He didn't show any real characteristics of somebody who had been ejected from a rollover vehicle. He had very minor amounts of dirt upon his person." What dirt he did have on his body was located mostly on his rear-end, suggesting he had scooted down the hill on his backside rather than been thrown from the truck.

Schilling said that from looking at the scene, it appeared that the truck could have easily made the turn, even if the brakes had failed, and that the "natural reaction" would have been to steer into the hillside rather than go through the barrier. Schilling believed that the truck probably hit the guardrail at about a 60- to 90-degree angle, crashed through and landed about 100 feet down the hill, then tumbled another few hundred feet. Even if Bergna couldn't steer into the hillside, the laws of physics prevented him from being thrown out the window and landing so far up the slope from where the truck crashed. He explained that a body in motion will stay in motion—in that same direction. "If you strike the guardrail at a sixty-degree angle on the passenger side of the vehicle, you are going to tend to want to go towards the passenger side and/or more towards the right front corner of the vehicle," he said.

"Not where you want to go?" asked Clifton.

"What is going to happen, based on physics, you have no control over it. You are not going to be ejected out the driver's window."

And quickly. A car traveling just 30 miles per hour translates to 45 feet *per second*—one second and Bergna would have been way, way down that hill.

He said the baseball cap that had been found at the scene also would have traveled in the direction of the passenger side—to the right—and continued along with the truck, and not somehow ended up on the pavement to the left.

"I have concluded I don't believe that he was in the vehicle when the vehicle went over the guardrail or through the guardrail and over the cliff," said Schilling.

"How certain are you of that conclusion?" asked Clifton.

"I am extremely. I would say about one hundred percent certain."

And so was the grand jury. After ten minutes of discussion, it issued an indictment:

The defendant PETER MATTHEW BERGNA is accused by the Washoe County, State of Nevada, of the following:

MURDER, a violation of NRS 200.010 and NRS 200.030, a felony, committed as follows:

That the said defendant on or between the 31st day of May A.D. 1998, and the 1st day of June A.D. 1998, or thereabout, at the County of Washoe, state of Nevada, did willfully, unlawfully, and with malice aforethought, deliberation, and premeditation, kill and murder RINETTE LOUISE RIELLA-BERGNA, a human being, by means of causing a vehicle in which she was a passenger to be driven

at, into and through a certain guardrail and over a
cliff or extremely steep embankment, thereby in-
flicting mortal injuries upon the said RINETTE
LOUISE RIELLA-BERGNA from which she died
on or about June 1, 1998.

Dated this 15th day of November, 2000.

It was signed by David W. Clifton, chief deputy district attorney, and by the foreman of the grand jury.

Two-and-a-half years after the accident on Slide
Mountain, it was time to arrest Peter Bergna.

Chapter 28

"Peter is innocent." Louis Bergna was speaking to his hometown paper, the *San Jose Mercury News*, in November 2000. "This was a horrible accident," the elder Bergna said. "We all loved Peter's wife Rinette very much, and we know that he wouldn't do anything to hurt her." As he spoke, his son sat in a Seattle jail cell awaiting extradition to Nevada.

Following Peter's indictment, Washoe District Judge Connie Steinheimer issued a no-bail warrant for his arrest. On November 17, 2000, Washoe County Sheriff's Detective Larry Canfield and Nevada Highway Patrol Trooper John Schilling joined police officers from Seattle in going to an address on Queen Anne Hill in Seattle, where they arrested Bergna without incident. Bergna remained in jail for five days without bail while he and his attorney mulled over whether to fight extradition to Nevada. When the King County, Washington, judge reduced his bail to $300,000—an amount Bergna and his family could easily raise—he gave up the extradition fight, bailed out of jail and returned to face the murder charge in Reno.

The case that had barely registered a blip on the news radar when Bergna's truck went flying off the cliff was now front-page news in Reno and a story of great interest in Santa Clara County. The Associated Press also began regular coverage, as did the local Reno television stations. Before it was all over, the case would be the subject of a *48 Hours* piece on CBS and a story in *People* magazine.

With the news media now interested, Washoe County, Nevada, authorities began waging more than just a legal offensive against Peter Bergna. Assistant DA Dave Clifton was quoted everywhere about the details of the case, disclosing everything from the pre-crash argument on the mountain about Rinette's long absences, to what he characterized as Bergna's changing stories about how the accident had occurred. He told the media—and thus many potential trial jurors—that Bergna's injuries hadn't matched the circumstances of the accident, that the highway patrol had found no skid marks and that Bergna had received a $450,000 insurance payout and a $275,000 inheritance settlement from Rinette's family. Bergna's camp also went public. "It took them two-and-a-half years to investigate an accident to come up with this charge," his lawyer, Frederick Pinkerton, told the press. "Mr. Bergna has cooperated thoroughly with the investigation, lengthy though it is. Now the case is indicted—we're going to fight." And Bergna's friend, Tim Gravett, expressed shock at his arrest: "We were with Peter the next morning after the accident and he was really just devastated. I was watching him when his mom got there the next day. He just went to her and hugged her and broke down in her arms. That says a lot right there. . . . He was overcome with grief."

More quietly, the Riella family instructed their attorney to end the civil case against Bergna. "They're going ahead with the criminal case," Rick recalled telling his lawyers. "Just get it over with." The family wrapped up its negotiations with Bergna's insurance company, receiving a $220,000 payout, and then dropped any claims against Bergna personally.

On November 29—twelve days after his arrest—Peter Bergna appeared before Washoe District Judge Brent Adams. Bergna was now 47 years old, his close-cropped hair receding, his eyes dark under his heavy eyebrows. He wore a dark suit and white shirt and tie. His parents, Louis and Pat, sat in the audience.

"Mr. Bergna," asked Adams, a distinguished-looking, silver-haired jurist right out of central casting, "how do you plead to the charge of murder as alleged in the indictment?"

"Not guilty," said Bergna.

"Thank you," said Adams. "The defendant's not guilty plea is entered."

And thus began a legal odyssey that would be almost as long as the one that had brought Bergna to court. Peter Bergna would spend much of the next two years staring at the marbled wall behind Adams in the downtown Reno courthouse. This case which would center on marriage that ended so violently would be played out across the street from the offices of the "Heart of Reno Wedding Chapel," which offered "certified legal marriages." Downstairs from Adams' court, young couples lined up at the clerk's office for marriage licenses.

After the plea was entered, lawyers discussed a trial date, with Clifton pressing. "The state would like a trial as soon as possible," he said. "We do not waive the right to speedy trial."

The judge asked Bergna lawyer Pinkerton, "Do you believe that it is unlikely, if not impossible, that there will be any plea bargain agreement, so therefore, certainly the case will be tried?"

"At this point it definitely is going to be tried, Your Honor," said Pinkerton. "I think there's been some violations of the laws of physics to support what I'm reading about [prosecution] theory. So we have a case here that is one, circumstantial, two, is ripe for a lot of expert study as well as testimony."

The lawyers then argued over whether Bergna should be freed on bail while awaiting trial, with Pinkerton predictably calling for bail. "If there was ever a time to flee, it would have been during that two-and-a-half-year period," Pinkerton said. "He could have sold all his assets off, taken the money and he could have gotten a long, long way in two-and-a-half years. He has remained available. He gave interviews to the police. His whereabouts have been informed to the authorities. He has in fact been waiting and waiting and waiting to see when, if, anything was going to take place."

Pinkerton suggested that the average bail for defendants facing murder charges in Northern Nevada was $250,000—and he questioned prosecutors' motives in seeking anything higher. "What I see going on here is an effort to try to stigmatize the defendant, beyond the simple fact that he's been indicted," he said. "I mean a no-bail warrant on a man that has been waiting for the charge, if there was going to be a charge, for two-and-a-half years? So we are asking Your Honor to set a reasonable bail and we will post it." He added that Bergna could also pledge his home in Incline Village, which had been appraised at $500,000.

Clifton countered that the state was "vehemently opposed to any bail." He said if any bail were granted, "We would adamantly ask Your Honor to impose extensive cash bail in the neighborhood of one million dollars. Make it cash only. Certainly not a property bond." Clifton said that, despite the defense's claims, bail is not common in murder cases. He said that in forty to fifty murder cases he knew of in Northern Nevada, only two had had bail offered to a defendant—and one of those men skipped bail during deliberations before he was found in Salt Lake City.

To argue for no bail, Clifton needed to show the judge that the prosecution had a strong case. And so, for the first time publicly, Clifton laid it out in detail.

Going into the couple's background, Clifton told the judge that Bergna and his wife were married "for some time," had no children, and that Mrs. Bergna was employed as a tour guide, much to Bergna's chagrin. "Mr. Bergna was getting highly agitated as to her travel and being gone so much, and her decision not to have children, even though she was currently forty-nine years of age at the time of her death," said Clifton. Bergna, according to the prosecutor, told people how unhappy he was with his wife's long absences and that "he desperately wants a wife that will stay at home more and have children with him."

On the night of Rinette's death, Peter Bergna had filled up two gas cans, but left part of the caps off, picked her up at the airport, driven to the side of Slide Mountain, parked the truck, smoked a cigar, then proceeded to drive his truck off the mountain, explaining later that the brakes had gone out.

"Does the vehicle have what is known as the ABS braking system?" the judge asked.

"Yes," Clifton said, "and all lines in that vehicle were still intact. There was no severed brake line at all." There were, in short, no signs that Bergna had tried to brake at all: The truck was found still in drive, the emergency brake had not been depressed, there were no swerve marks on the roadway, no skid marks.

"Was there any evidence concerning the speed at the time the vehicle left the roadway?" the judge asked.

"Yes, twenty-two miles per hour when it went off the cliff."

Clifton said that, under the prosecution's theory, the truck went through the guardrail at a sharp angle—60 to 90 degrees. He said that to do that, the truck had to have turned left at first while going down the hill to negotiate the left-bending turn, then made a sharp right to go nearly straight into the guardrail, and off the mountain, leaving a thirteen-foot gap in the rail, not wide enough for the big truck to go through sideways.

"What was the extent of injuries?" the judge asked.

"He had no injuries consistent with going down the hill [and being] ejected," said Clifton. "There was no leaves or twigs or anything like that upon his hair or person, no scrapes, abrasions or scratches. He had a broken or severely sprained ankle. What happens is, he got out of the vehicle voluntarily and landed on his feet with his right foot rolling over in the direction the car is traveling."

"Did he say anything about his or his wife's use of seatbelts?"

"He did not have his on. She did. He admitted he turned her airbag off because of her stature. He felt it would be dangerous to have an airbag on the passenger because of her size. His airbag did deploy."

"What is her stature?"

"Very small. Under five feet. A little heavy for her stature."

"Where was he when the emergency vehicle arrived on the scene?"

"Eighty feet down, less than the point of impact of the vehicle."

Clifton argued that what little damage there was to Bergna's body and clothing was caused by the man jumping out of the truck while it was still on the roadway, hitting his head on the door, landing on his feet and spraining his ankle. The side of his right shoe—the foot that was injured—was scuffed with asphalt, the prosecutor said. Bergna then scampered down the hill on his behind and dialed 911 on his cell phone, said Clifton. "The transport nurse in the Care Flight helicopter with him says it was highly unusual, very strange that this man was screaming on and on about his wife but had no tears," the prosecutor said.

The judge asked if Rinette was killed by the accident. Clifton said that that was the case, with no evidence of any other injuries being administered before the accident, and that the time of death appeared to have been about 1 a.m.

As for a motive, Clifton said bank employee Leo Humphreys told police that about two weeks before the accident, while Rinette was in Europe, Bergna had asked Humphreys about a "very good-looking blonde" who also worked there. Humphreys claimed he'd told Bergna, "I can't get involved with that. You want to date her, you call her on your own." That same day, Bergna did in fact call the tall, slender blonde and asked her out to the movies. The judge asked if there would be evidence of infidelity. "No," Clifton conceded, "and I agree Mr. Bergna has good credentials. And that is why this is going to trial."

"You indicated as to motive, there's evidence concerning the advantage to Mr. Bergna from his wife's death as opposed to divorce?"

"In the nature of approximately one million dollars, easily," said Clifton. "The motive, Your Honor, is not even entirely financial. And I've always told Mr. Pinkerton that. This was almost a spur-of-the-moment–type thing, when he must have decided while she was in Italy that he's better off killing her than if they have to go through divorce or remain married, and he can't have children and she's never home."

As for bail, Clifton said prosecutors were not worried Bergna would flee—yet. With bravado, the prosecutor said: "This is the first time Mr. Pinkerton and Mr. Bergna have heard my theory of our case—that he jumped out of the vehicle himself, and planned to do it. . . . They are now hearing the strength of the state's case, so now he may or may not get a little worried by our case."

As impressed as Clifton was with his case, Bergna didn't exactly try to make a run for it just then. Rather, Pinkerton sought to dismantle the prosecution's circumstantial case, starting with what he called the illogical motive. "What I understand to be the motive here is that Mr. Bergna wanted to spend more time with his wife. That hardly sounds like a motive to then kill her."

Noting that some of the evidence against Bergna came from his own police interview, Pinkerton suggested that Bergna's statements should be seen in light of the circumstances, including the fact that Bergna's father had encouraged lots of cooperation. "It was lengthy, extended only because Mr. [Lou] Bergna insisted that [Peter] Bergna continue to talk to them," said Pinkerton. "[He] is still suffering from the accident. He still is in shock. He's in trauma, and trying to answer the questions that Mr. Clifton is indicating somehow ought to be evaluated with a cool head—somebody who has had time to think about things, organize thoughts, so they can respond intelligently. It's just a scattering of phrases."

The evidence, Pinkerton said, also showed no premeditation. "Have you ever heard of anyone putting themselves at risk of dying in order to kill someone else?" he asked. "He had to be driving that truck and make a turn while trying to get out. Now, I've known Peter Bergna for two-and-a-half years, now. He's not athletic. That is a good move even for an athlete." He said of the 911 tape, "This is not the voice of a man who has coolly performed anything."

Asked by the judge about the prosecution's evidence of no signs of braking, Pinkerton alluded to problems Ford has had with brakes in some of its trucks.

The cellular phone that just happened to be in Peter's hand? He needed to have it at the airport in case his wife had to call with a change in plans.

The lack of tears? "Absolute nonsense."

Bergna's minor injuries? Pinkerton didn't offer an explanation, but did home back in on the motive evidence, blasting Clifton's inference that Bergna's asking about the blonde had sinister overtones. "By the way," Pinkerton said, "as part of his business, he takes female clients to dinner and asks them out. It's been part of his routine or business for years and years and years. It doesn't signify he has any raging infidelity or affair going on. Not at all. That's just the way he conducts his business."

A possible marital rift over children? "Mr. Bergna did indeed want to have children. Mrs. Bergna wanted to pursue her overseas travel," acknowledged Pinkerton. "This is the type of thing a husband and wife talk about."

The judge then asked Pinkerton about why Bergna didn't just steer his way out of danger. "He's turning the vehicle at a guardrail, knowing that there's a seven-hundred-foot cliff on the other side. Why would he do that?" asked Adams. "He jumps out before the vehicle goes over the side. [That] is the state's theory."

"I know what their theory is," said Pinkerton. "It's obvious the truck hit the guardrail and there's residue from the airbag on him, on Mr. Bergna."

"What about residue not consistent with airbag?" the judge asked, inquiring if some other material could have been left on Bergna that just looked like airbag residue.

"I'm unaware of any other source that would produce that type of material," said Pinkerton. But Clifton said he was: "Material starch from dry cleaner," he suggested.

Finally, the judge asked about whether the prosecution intended to seek the death penalty against Bergna.

"We may go to death penalty on it," said Clifton. "He doesn't have a record, but he did kill his wife." Clifton said his office would have a decision in about two weeks.

The judge then asked for financial documents listing Bergna's assets, and said he would read the grand jury transcript before making a decision on bail. In the meantime, Bergna would remain free on the bail granted in Washington state.

Three days later, on December 1, 2000, Judge Brent Adams issued a written ruling: "The court hereby finds that the proof is evident and the presumption is great that the defendant committed the offense charged." He denied bail for Peter Bergna, who would now be locked up until his trial began, meaning months behind bars. The only good news for Bergna was that he wouldn't be sitting in jail under a death cloud. On January 17, 2001, Clifton announced that the DA's office would not seek the death penalty. By now, Bergna had ditched the lawyer who'd lost the bail hearing and hired new counsel, Michael Schwartz of Seattle, who would speak of Bergna's mindset: "I think the greatest burden for him to bear is to think that there are people who think he's guilty of killing his wife, that people consider this to be something other than the horrific accident that it was."

Chapter 29

The new lawyer brought a new aggressiveness to Peter Bergna's defense. On March 9, 2001, with Bergna in jail now for three months, attorney Michael Schwartz, a former prosecutor in Washington state, made his first appearance before Judge Adams. Schwartz would have two other lawyers on the team: David Smith of Seattle and Roberto Puentes of Reno.

"Thank you, Your Honor, may it please the court and counsel and, in preparatory remarks, I would like to thank the court for the honor and privilege of appearing in this case."

"I notice you are from Seattle," said the judge. "You're not related to Irwin Schwartz, are you?"

"I'm not."

"Is he still practicing?"

"Not as much as he used to—not for a number of years."

And with those introductory pleasantries, Schwartz

got down to it: trying to convince Adams to throw out the indictment against Bergna on the grounds that an inappropriate presentation had been made before the grand jury, with improper evidence provided and potentially exonerating evidence withheld. It was a bold move, as the judge himself noted. "I can't think of any instance in my limited experience in state or federal court where the presiding judge has been called upon" to overturn a grand jury's decision, he said. Schwartz quickly responded that there was "nothing in the statute to prevent it." He went on to blast the prosecution's presentation to the grand jury as failing to meet even the low-level standard of proof needed to secure a grand jury indictment.

"Speculation is not considered evidence," said Schwartz. "We are not allowed to speculate."

He said prosecutors had withheld information showing that cornstarch was found on Bergna's clothing. He claimed the starch on the clothing would be a sign that Bergna had been in the truck when the airbag deployed— upon impact with the cliff. "By withholding [this] from the grand jury . . . they never had an opportunity to make an independent judgment," said Schwartz.

Also, he said, the jury only heard half the 911 call, when Bergna sounded much more composed than he did in the beginning of the call, when he was frantically yelling for Rinette and had to be constantly quieted by the patient dispatcher. They didn't hear the police interviews—only Beltron's characterization of them. What they did hear, Schwartz said, was a lot of improper testimony from women about how Bergna behaved at the retirement party. "Its only purpose was entirely prejudicial, and that is to portray Mr. Bergna as something less than an honorable individual," said Schwartz. And, he accused investigators of "rigging" a reconstruction of the accident to make it look like Bergna intentionally steered the truck into the guardrail. "The truck they were testing consistently veered to the right, two or three or four times. Eventually they moved the wheels over the center line and—rigging the test that way—they got the truck to veer left," said Schwartz. "You can hear [in a videotape] Trooper Schilling in one of the more amusing parts of the re-enactment say, 'That's more like it.'"

Finally, Schwartz said that Schilling had made himself out to be more of an accident reconstruction expert than he really was. Schilling only twice attended two-week training sessions on accident reconstruction. "But it does not make him an expert on accident reconstruction. Trooper Schilling is not an expert on guardrail construction." This lack of expertise, Schwartz said, undercuts Schilling's theory that Bergna didn't have the kind of injuries or was dirty enough to have been expelled from the truck upon impact of the cliff. "That is pure unadulterated speculation. How somebody can say this is enough dirt or not enough dirt is beyond me," said Schwartz. Schilling said he was "near one hundred percent certain that Peter Bergna was not in the truck when it left the road surface," according to Schwartz. "It's the linchpin of their case," he said. "But if Mr. Bergna has cornstarch from deployment of the airbag, then Mr. Bergna had to have been in the car when it happened."

Prosecutor Dave Clifton agreed with the judge that it was almost unheard of in Nevada to seek the dismissal of a grand jury indictment. "There is no such thing as a completely errorless trial and I will agree, your honor, there were a few mistakes. I will I agree I made a mistake or two," he said. "But the important issue is: They are not the death knell to this criminal indictment for murder." He said the legal standard was whether the indictment was "legally sufficient"—and he argued it was. "There is no law that says if they didn't receive the best legal evidence that you throw out the indictment," he said. "You don't come back and second-guess the grand jury."

Clifton called the cornstarch argument a "red herring." He said the cornstarch on the clothing hadn't been proven to be connected to the airbag in the truck—or any airbag. "Even with an airbag, he'd be dead and he would have gone all the way to the bottom."

Asked by the judge why he didn't play the tape of the police interview, Clifton said there was an issue with the mention of a polygraph. "He didn't pass the polygraph. He didn't flunk it either," the prosecutor said. "But he was breathing so intentionally or exhaustively when he was asked important questions that the polygrapher put in his report: 'I could not make an ethical conclusion as to the result of this polygraph because of the intentional breathing patterns during important questions even though he was admonished not to do to that.'"

A week after the hearing, Adams issued a one-page ruling: "The court finds that the evidence received at the grand jury proceeding . . . establishes probable cause to believe that the charged offense was committed and that petitioner committed it." The indictment would stand. But having heard Schwartz's vigorous defense, Clifton now knew he was in for a battle. He told the local newspaper: "There are no eyewitnesses to the crime. It is a circumstantial case, so there will be plenty of arguments remaining as to what each item of evidence means to either side, and we expect there will be more motions and more legal maneuvering prior to the trial."

It was a battle that Peter Bergna's father would not see to its conclusion. Just days after this decision, Louis Bergna collapsed on a golf course. Two days later, on March 22, 2001, he died of a heart ailment at Santa Teresa Community Hospital in South San Jose. He was 79. "We regarded him more as a personal hero than as a boss," Assistant District Attorney Tom Fahrenholz, who had been hired by Bergna nearly three decades earlier, told the *San Jose Mercury News*. "He was just incorruptible and never played favorites," said San Jose lawyer James McManis, who got his start working for Bergna. "His instruction to all new deputies was to do the right thing. If a deputy felt that any case should not be prosecuted, that was good enough for the boss." As for his son Peter, sitting in a Washoe County jail awaiting a murder trial, "He believed devoutly in the innocence of his son," retired Superior Court Judge James A. Wright, who had known Lou Bergna for sixty years, told the San Jose newspaper, "and he certainly was affected by the charges, but he did not waver one inch from his belief in his son's innocence."

Chapter 30

The case that had taken so long to get to court was now barreling toward a trial, and much work for both sides needed to be done over the summer so they would be ready in the fall. For the prosecution, lab work was being completed in late May and early June 2001 on the most important physical evidence in the case Scott Stoeffler, a microbiologist and chemist at McCrone Associates Laboratory in Chicago, examined black smudges on Peter Bergna's size 10½ Comfort Plus canvas shoes. Specifically, the prosecution wanted to make sure that the smudges on the right shoe came from asphalt. Stoeffler used a solvent that would dissolve asphalt if it were present, and it did just that. The stain then was examined using infrared spectroscopy, which measures the frequency of infrared light that a material absorbs to see if the stain was made up of asphalt's key ingredients: carbon, hydrogen and sulphur. This test did find those elements, along with mineral clays, quartz, feldspar—all consistent with the makeup of asphalt. Stoeffler also found apparent asphalt on a stain on Bergna's sock, on streaks on his jacket sleeve and stains on a piece of snap on the jacket in the hip area. There were no signs of asphalt on the Levi's. What's more, he found no plant-like material on the shoes, socks, jacket or pants that would arguably have been present if he had been thrown into the hillside.

Stoeffler also examined the cornstarch on Bergna's blue jeans and jacket. The samples were sent to him by the Washoe County crime lab that had collected them; the samples were on electrostatic lifts, thin pieces of film used to pick up dust and debris. Working in his lab's filtered dust-free "clean room," Stoeffler found plant grains on the electrostatic lift from the Levi's and on the jacket. Most of the grains appeared to be cornstarch, the others appeared to be another kind of starch, probably wheat. His conclusion: "The numbers of starch grains that was off the lifts would not be unusual to see from an ordinary environmental dust sample. Some environmental dust samples might even have more, some would have less, depending on the particular place they were taken from, but I would not call those numbers unusual." He attempted to find out whether these cornstarch grains matched those used in the protective shield on the airbag in Bergna's truck, but, he said, "I couldn't tell where the grains came from." Cornstarch grains are all alike—no matter where they're used.

Bergna's defense also tied up its loose ends, hiring an expert witness, engineer Lindley Manning, who would testify that Trooper Schilling lacked the educational level, particularly in calculus level math, to come up with the conclusion that the truck had hit the guardrail at a near–right angle after Bergna bailed out. Manning would argue that somebody with a higher level of education would know that Bergna instead had to have been thrown from the window.

The defense also filed papers seeking to bar from the

jury recorded statements by Bergna to police after the crash, contending that police lied to Bergna about the caretaker and other issues, and that Bergna was under the influence of medication and not thinking clearly. Finally, the defense wanted to throw out the testimony of two of the women whom Bergna allegedly flirted with before and after the crash. Judge Adams considered the defense's evidentiary issues at a hearing, where the prosecution called the two women to the stand, starting with Brenda Redl-Harge, who told the judge about the surprise birthday party before the crash where she'd had to try to keep Bergna away from a friend, and spoke of the hot tub in the weeks after the crash.

"Did he touch your breasts?" asked prosecutor Dave Clifton.

"Yes," she said.

"Did you consent to that or tell him he could?"

"No I did not."

"And what reaction did it cause from you?"

"Panic."

"Did you have a discussion with him or anything or talk to him about it at that time?"

"I told him that I didn't want him to do that. He asked—He started to get mad, asked what was wrong and at that point I said I just wanted to go home."

"And he let you go and you left with your daughter, correct?"

"Right."

In Bergna's first chance to challenge this claim, a member of his defense team, attorney Roberto Puentes, asked, "Ms. Redl-Harge, being here today, is this exciting for you or embarrassing?"

"Scary, embarrassing."

"Scary?"

"A little bit of everything, I don't know what it is."

"You're scared of Mr. Bergna, aren't you? You're distrustive of him. It makes you nervous all along, the entire period you knew him?"

"Everything makes me nervous, yes."

"[On the] hot tub night, you were still distrustful or nervous being around Peter?"

"I was still a little nervous, yes."

"If you were mistrustful of him and wouldn't go see him without Teresa, why would you go to the house, let alone the hot tub?"

"No reason."

"You can't answer that?"

"There is no particular reason."

Puentes asked what she was wearing. She said she had on her bathing suit under shorts and a shirt.

"So you're distrustful of Mr. Bergna, nervous around him, but you drive up to Incline to have dinner, drink wine and a hot tub?"

"I did go, yes."

"You two are in the hot tub?"

"Yes."

"You've had some wine?"

"That is right."

"You're looking at the stars?"

"Yes."

"And apparently Mr. Bergna made a pass at you, for lack of a better phrase?"

"That is right."

"And you told him to stop?"

"Yes."

"And he did?"

"Yes."

After Redl-Harge finished testifying, the defense used a similar tactic with Janet Mello, the banker whom Bergna had called for a movie date.

"I don't want to offend you," said Puentes. "He didn't talk dirty to you?"

"No, nothing like that."

"He didn't pant on the phone?"

"No."

"He didn't try to call you after that?"

"No."

"When he made the call and asked about going to the movies, he didn't solicit in the intimate or sexual sense—anything like that?"

"No."

The last witness challenged by the defense was one of Bergna's neighbors, Cindy Glatz, who said that in winter 1997 or spring 1998 she saw Bergna shoot snow at his wife with a snow blower as she walked to her car. Glatz insisted that that Bergna clearly was not playing with his wife when he did this.

"How could you determine whether or not it was playful?" asked Clifton.

"My experience with snow blowers is that it's dangerous to be in the stream of snow. Objects and hard ice can injure people, and I could tell that she was not at all enjoying it."

"Did she laugh?"

"No, she did not."

During cross-examination, Puentes asked her, "You're married?"

"Yes, I am."

"Would you agree that couples argue?"

"Yes, sometimes."

"You argue with your husband, I'm sure?"

"Upon occasion."

"Two or three times per year maybe?"

"Probably."
"No further questions."

The hearing ended without a decision from the judge, who said he wanted to think about it, and signaled that he might not rule on some of these issues, including the testimony from the women, until the trial was under way. That meant that the defense had to prepare itself for the heart of the prosecution's case: the flirtation testimony, the accident reconstruction, and, perhaps most damaging, Peter Bergna's own words during the police interviews. There wasn't much time left now to prepare. The trial was one month away.

Chapter 31

The last time Peter Bergna had spoken, on the record, about the events that led to the death of his wife on Slide Mountain, it was in the police interviews, one taped, two videotaped, in which he spoke for hours. But now, having already spent ten months in jail and facing the very real possibility of dying there, the 48-year-old Bergna was careful with his words when he spoke out on the eve of his trial. "I've waited for my day in court to tell my side of the story for over two-and-a-half years," he told reporter Scott Sonner of the Associated Press on October 1, 2001, as jury selection began in the trial. "I'm an innocent man. I'm humble, but confident."

Bergna spoke during a courtroom break. He wore a charcoal pinstripe suit, blue dress shirt, navy tie and black wingtips. "I'm very nervous," he told Sonner, "but I believe I'm an innocent person and want to show that to the court and have my life back." And he spoke of his father, Louis Bergna, who had died just six months before. "I've always grown up in a system with a father who was a district attorney to know the system as being fair and honest," he said. "I hope it will be for me." As he spoke of missing his father's funeral, he wiped away tears—the tears that the prosecution would soon tell a jury he couldn't shed after the accident. "It was absolutely a horrific accident my wife and I were in. I love my wife to this day. It is unfair what happened to me and the fact I was unable to attend my father's funeral," he said. "But it is important the truth come out now and that people hear the whole story, not just what they want to make up. My father taught us kids to be honest and ethical and upstanding. It's all I've ever known." Time in jail, he said, was spent in prayer and reading the Bible. "I've been examining my own life," he said. "I came to the conclusion I have nothing to be guilty about. I have nothing to be afraid about."

Bergna expressed similar sentiments in a written statement to the *Reno Gazette-Journal*. "It really hurts that people would even think or believe that I would intentionally ever do anything to harm my wife," he wrote. "I loved this woman. I cherished her. We had an incredible marriage together." Rinette, he said, "gave me so much confidence and love and understanding, it was incredible. And every day for the rest of my life I will always think about her. I think that is what I probably miss most about her, is that unconditional love and trust." He said, "I miss this woman incredibly." As for her family, "I was very hurt when they informed me that they thought I staged the accident [as claimed in the wrongful death suit] because I always cared for them. In my Christian faith, I've forgiven them a long time ago."

Bergna's remarks about faith and family and innocence came as the first batch of prospective jurors was called into Judge Adams' courtroom. Whether those ultimately picked would ever hear him utter the same sentiments from the jury box remained to be seen, but by going to the media on the day jury selection began, Bergna was sure to reach at least some of those who would decide his fate. It was a cross-section of the Washoe County population that answered the call for jury duty—the retirees, teachers, office clerks and blackjack dealers sitting in Adams' court—to hear a speech about patriotism, a concept that had never been more in vogue than at this time in American history. The September 11 terrorist attack on the World Trade Center had occurred just three weeks earlier. Nerves were still jangled and faith in the American way was running at a new high. The prospective jurors listened as Adams applauded them for "demonstrating your good citizenship" by showing up for what looked to be "a very interesting case" with "superb lawyers on both sides." It was a sales pitch. The case was going to be long—about six weeks—and experience had shown Adams that people could think of plenty of other things to do than sit in his courtroom. "It is a very substantial commitment. Jury duty is a responsibility. It is not easy. It requires sacrifice," he told them. "But it is the only way our system can work. . . . No judge, no law, no Congress can make our system work unless you do."

The words seemed to have an effect. Despite a string of excuses, from back problems to pending vacations, a jury was selected in just three days, and on Thursday, October 4, 2001, the jurors sat, notebooks in their hands, and listened as Chief Deputy District Attorney Dave Clifton played an audiotape of a hysterical man on the side of a mountain. "My car is way down the hill. My wife's in the car," Peter Bergna says between sobs. "My wife, she's in the car." At the defense table, Bergna wiped tears as he heard his voice, but Clifton made it clear in his opening statements that the only tears that were ever shed the day that 49-year-old Rinette Riella-Bergna went off that cliff were crocodile tears. "There was a huge rift growing in their marriage," Clifton told the jurors, a rift that led Peter to fill up two gas cans and drive his wife up to a remote mountain aerie with evil intent. "To him, murder was the only way out, financially and emotionally." The prosecutor said Bergna had tried to explain what happened on the mountain, but that police didn't buy it—and neither would the jury after it saw the scientific evidence and heard Bergna's statements. Clifton made it clear that his most important witness was going to be one who might never take the stand, but whose words and demeanor would be presented before the jury. Clifton was seeking to nail Bergna with his own statements to authorities. "Was it real, or was it contrived?" he asked about Bergna's story. "The evidence will show you that what he claims is physically impossible. . . . He jumped out. This was planned."

In the defense opening, attorney Michael Schwartz borrowed the prosecution question and made it his own. "Is their case contrived or is it real? Is their case based on real evidence?" When the jury looks at this real evidence, he said, "The scientific analysis proves it was an accident." The prosecution case, he said, was a rush to judgment. "They arrived at a conclusion early, within six hours of the accident . . . based on assumptions," he said. "To this day, this case has been a conclusion in search of evidence." The defense case did have much going for it, with the lack of an eyewitness and a motive that was hardly compelling. Still, Schwartz's team faced an uphill battle, having lost so many pre-trial skirmishes from the bail hearing through the evidentiary hearing. The indictment wasn't thrown out and neither were the audio- and videotapes of Bergna's statements. The judge would also allow the testimony of the women whom Bergna was said to have hit on.

Still, Schwartz had before him all the makings of

a strong reasonable doubt defense. But he decided to go a step further, showing the jury a video animation—prosecutors would belittle it as a "cartoon"—that depicted the defense's theory of how the accident had occurred. It was a dramatic difference. Rather than having the truck slam into the guardrail at a near-right angle, the defense theory, as dramatized in the video, had the truck running alongside the guardrail, striking the post, then flying into the air with a twisting motion that flung Bergna out of the driver's-side window as it faced down toward the ground. This was the boldest step yet for the defense. Many attorneys present no defense at all, opting to instead chip away at the prosecution case through cross-examination, then argue at the end that the state had failed to meet its burden. Now Bergna's defense had gone pro-active by presenting an alternative scenario rather than just showing problems with the prosecution's theory. The upside was that if the jury believed the defense theory of the crash, Bergna would be a free man. The downside was that by putting on so affirmative a defense, Bergna's team risked having the prosecution do to the defense what the defense normally does to the prosecution: go on the attack.

The prosecution opened its case in chief by bringing jurors back to the night of the crash, calling emergency workers to talk about their surprise at how little injury Bergna suffered—and how little emotion he seemed to show after the crash. Firefighter/paramedic Jeff Sambrano described for jurors how he'd scurried down the hill on a safety line to find—to his surprise—that Bergna was unharmed, save for some pain in his ankle and lower back, and that even his clothes were not particularly damaged.

During cross-examination, Roberto Puentes sought to

show that Sambrano, like others, may have misinter-preted what they saw.

"You ever hear a story, sir, where for instance, a baby falls out of a two-story building and doesn't get injured?" asked Puentes.

"Sure. Absolutely."

"Ever watch *Real TV* where there's ejection and the person walks away uninjured?"

"Sure. Absolutely."

"Ever hear about maybe an airplane crash where everybody dies except for one person?"

"Not too often, but I'm sure it's happened."

On redirect examination by Clifton, Sambrano still said he was surprised. He didn't even start an IV because there seemed to be no need for it. "I think the thing that kind of was, again, poking me in the eye for lack of a bet-ter way to put it, was the patient was, basically, uninjured. The clothes weren't severely damaged, there were no sig-nificant injuries. The patient didn't seem very emotional [over] what happened, and the patient had a cell phone."

Helicopter Care Flight nurse, Phyllis Tejeda, echoed Sambrano's surpise at the apparent lack of emotion by Bergna. "He was crying, 'My wife, my wife,' that kind of stuff," she said under questioning by Clifton. "But . . . he didn't have any tears, so of course, I'm a little alarmed that he doesn't have any tears, because people—children especially—when they're very dehydrated or in shock, they can cry dry tears." But, she said, he wasn't a child and he wasn't in shock. "It clued me in, just another clue as to something's not right here."

About the only things she did deal with were his com-plaints of ankle pain, for which she gave him the mor-phine, and the apparent anxiety manifested by the sobs and the elevated blood pressure, for which she gave him the sedative.

"If he were to have just killed somebody, such as his wife, could that cause anxiety?" asked Clifton.

"I would hope so," she said.

"So could the elevated signs that you indicated a moment ago be caused by something like that?"

She didn't get out an answer because the judge sustained a defense objection to the question. During cross-examination, defense lawyer David Smith tried to explain away the missing tears.

"Could a person be cried out?" he asked.

"Yeah," said Tejeda, but then she added, "I've never seen it happen."

"OK."

"I've never seen that happen to an adult. With children, it's due to severe dehydration."

Chapter 32

It was just the second day of testimony, in what would be a long trial, but the case was about to enter an important stage for both the prosecution and the defense. The morning of Friday, October 5, 2001, began normally enough, with the defense agreeing to let jurors see a detailed plaster model that a hobby enthusiast had made depicting the side of Slide Mountain with the little road from which the truck went off the cliff. Although Schwartz accepted the model, he did so grudgingly. "I suppose just for the most rudimentary of illustrative purposes, we'll not object to its admission," he said, in a sign of a rough-and-tumble fight that was to come.

After Nevada Highway Patrol Trooper Rick McLellan took the stand to talk about the night he found Bergna lying on the hillside with few injuries and, up on the roadway, none of the usual signs of such an accident—"No skid marks, no turn marks, and I found that odd," he said—the prosecution called Trooper John Schilling. With the judge having rejected the defense objection to

Schilling's testimony, the trooper went up to the plaster model of the mountain and proceeded to lay out his theory of how the accident occurred. He said that "the accident I investigated" bore little resemblance to the one illustrated in opening statements by the defense's animated video. Testifying in great detail over four hours that first day, Schilling said he and others re-enacted the accident on the mountain and could not do it the way Bergna's defense said it was done, with the truck running alongside the guardrail rather than coming straight at it. "I took a Ford pickup up the hill at about twenty-five miles per hour, came down that guardrail and attempted to make the turn into it, and it's literally impossible to get to that area of impact at twenty-five miles per hour without striking the guardrail upstream further. I just couldn't make the turn."

And even if it did manage to hit the rail and post at the angle the defense said it did, it would have been impossible for the truck to spin as quickly and sharply as the defense claimed, Schilling said. "In the video, the vehicle strikes the pole, begins a clockwise rotation, [and] started down mountain," Schilling said. "[That] literally takes away its forward momentum. A vehicle is going to tend to stay in a straight line unless something else acts upon it, but if it does hit something, the rotation that you're going to have is going to be a counterclockwise rotation." In other words, the truck would be spinning in such a way that Bergna wouldn't be thrown from the window and down onto the hillside, but instead he would be thrown into the passenger seat—and smack into the seatbelted Rinette.

As important as Schilling's reconstruction of the accident was to the prosecution, his testimony would become eye-glazingly technical, and jurors seemed to lose concentration as he launched into long-winded answers. One doozy went this way: "The principle direction of force not only can cause rotation, but it can also cause occupant movement, and when you're talking about occupant movement, they talk about it being opposite from and parallel from principle direction of force, so if the force is coming this way, the occupant's going to move opposite the force and parallel to it, so it's going to force him more in this scenario. If it strikes and it's this direction, then it's going to force him more forward and to the right."

After a weekend respite, Schilling returned to the stand on Monday for day two of his testimony, insisting it was entirely possible—and likely—for Bergna to have jumped out of the truck before it went off the cliff. "I was involved in a pursuit in Las Vegas where I was chasing a Camaro through the city streets, and after I made the first right-hand turn, the two occupants jumped out and immediately went down on their face and the vehicle subsequently crashed," he said. "And prior to me getting back to them, they ran and I never caught them."

"How fast were you going during the chase?" asked Clifton.

"Over twenty miles per hour when we made the corner"—about the same speed that authorities estimated Bergna's truck was traveling.

Although the judge deemed Schilling a relevant witness, that didn't stop Schwartz from repeating in front of the jury what he had argued before the trial in front of the judge: that Schilling wasn't qualified to make the claims he did. When Schilling once again dismissed the plausibility of the defense's animated video simulating the crash, Schwartz snapped, "Well, it's clear that you don't understand the mechanics, the math, the physics."

"Objection, Your Honor," Clifton said. "Argumentative."

But the judge allowed the defense some leeway to

challenge Schilling's credentials. "Please finish the question," said Adams.

"It's clear to you," Schwartz continued, "that you do not understand the math and physical science that goes behind the defense's theory of this accident?"

"I don't know how they perform their calculations, correct."

"You're essentially telling us that you don't understand what you don't understand, right?"

But Schilling fought on. "I don't understand what mathematics they used in producing the video that we showed," he said. "I do know by personal experience that the video that was shown, that you cannot round that corner and stay that close to the guardrail at a speed they are portraying it at. And I also know that as the vehicle strikes . . . the guardrail and begins its turn or clockwise rotation, that that forward momentum that I talked about before no longer is there and the vehicle merely drives down the mountainside."

But Schwartz suggested that this personal experience—the September 1999 reenactment on the mountainside—was flawed. The lawyer played the videotape of the reenactment and pointed out that at one spot a trooper can be heard saying, "This is a little more promising."

"What exactly does that mean, Trooper?"

"I believe that he was talking about how the super elevation would react to the pickup truck."

"So you went up there actually attempting to accomplish a particular result?"

"No. I think we went up there to do specific tests."

The defense lawyer then began quizzing the trooper on his knowledge of physics, beginning with something called the "fall formula" and the variables that could be used with it.

"How about this one: The fall formula is based on the object that you're calculating being literally a particle like a round little pebble, right?" the lawyer asked.

"I haven't been told that in any of my training classes," Schilling said.

"OK. So if it were true that the fall formula is based on a particle that has no mass and that the application of the fall formula to an object such as a forty-seven-hundred-pound truck which does obviously have a great deal of mass . . ."

"OK," Schilling said blankly.

". . . there would be some changes or differences or some kind of approximating being done, correct?"

"In all the training classes I've been to, I've never been given that scenario, so I don't think I really have an answer."

He didn't have an answer, the defense lawyer suggested, because his level of training fell woefully short.

"Level of knowledge," said Schwartz. "Well, let's talk about yours. In high school, what was the highest level course in math that you took?"

"I completed geometry."

"And any physics courses?"

"No."

"Any engineering courses?"

"No."

"In the period of time that you were in college, did you take any math classes?"

"No, I did not."

"Physics?"

"No."

"Engineering?"

"No."

He also acknowledged that when he testified at the

grand jury about using Newton's first law of physics to formulate his theory of the crash, what he really meant to say was Newton's third law of physics.

"You have a theory, right?"

"Yes."

"You never tested it, correct?"

"I did not do calculations, no."

"So as you stand here or sit here today, you have no idea whether it's physically possible your theory is correct?"

"I believe it to be physically possible."

"I know what you believe," he said sarcastically, prompting a sharp reply from Clifton, who said, "Objection Your Honor!" even as Schilling started to answer the question.

"One person at a time," the judge said.

"I do not have math behind it to back it up, no," the trooper said.

The assault would go into the next day, Schilling's third day on the stand, with Schwartz showing the defense video again and asking, "How many degrees of freedom or degrees of motion are described by what's going on here?"

"I don't know."

"Isn't that one of the laws of physics?"

"Sure, could be. I don't know."

On the issue of Bergna's ejection from the truck, Schwartz hammered on Schilling's theory that the scuff marks on his shoes were evidence that he jumped out of the car onto the pavement.

"Trooper, you're not an expert on shoe scuffs, are you?"

"No, I'm not."

"Do you have any background in forensic examination that would allow you to even render an opinion about what the marks on the shoes indicate?"

"No, but I have seen people who have. I've seen road rash on people."

As the cross-examination wore on, Schwartz suggested repeatedly that what he was hoping the jury would see was that the ill-informed, under-educated Schilling came to a conclusion about how the accident occurred and then backtracked, using what limited knowledge he had to back it up.

"So, Trooper, there is no evidence that could be presented to you that would change your mind about this truck and how it headed down the mountain? Right?"

"Your Honor, he asked that over and over again," Clifton complained.

"Sustained," the judge said wearily.

"Is there anything that could ever occur to convince you that you're wrong?"

"I based my conclusions off of the totality of my investigation and, based upon my training and experience, I believe my conclusions to be correct. So I would say, No."

That wouldn't be the end of it. The next day, Schilling's fourth on the stand, the defense grilling continued, then the prosecution tried again to show that Schilling was right and the defense video was wrong, then back again to cross-examination, until the jury was obviously weary of the entire exercise.

Both sides, however, seemed to get what they wanted: the prosecution built the first pillar of its case, outlining why it believed the truck had gone in at a near–right angle toward the guardrail as Bergna bailed out; the defense made its point that Schilling had based this theory on arguably shaky academic grounds. It wouldn't be the end of the drawn-out bickering and analysis of what had transpired in those few violent seconds in the middle of the night. Nor, it turned out, would it be the most antagonistic stretch of the case. Later that day, after Schilling left the stand, the prosecution set out to build the second pillar of its case, playing the police interviews of Bergna for the jury to allow Bergna to hurt himself.

But a shock was awaiting—one that threatened to derail the entire trial.

Chapter 33

It all began smoothly enough for the prosecution. After ER nurse Jeanine Moorhead spoke of how she never saw Bergna cry while he made his phone call to a friend, lamenting, "It's horrible, it's horrible," after the accident, the prosecution called Washoe County Sheriff's Sergeant James Beltron. Although he would be called to describe some of the details of the night of the crash, including Bergna's puzzling return to the scene—while his wife lay dead in the street in a body bag—to retrieve his fanny pack, Beltron's main purpose was to be a legal vehicle by which the prosecution would introduce into evidence the tapes of Bergna's police interviews. As such, Beltron recounted how the four cops had gone to Bergna's house and how Bergna had voluntarily hobbled on crutches with them to the substation a couple miles away for the first interview.

"Did you see any signs or obvious signs of any type of reactions to medication that he may have been taking?" asked Clifton.

"His speech was clear, and I saw no indication of—that I could pick up—he was impaired in any way," said Beltron.

"Were you able to understand his answers? Was he making sense?"

"Yes he was."

"How did the interview terminate? Do you recall?"

"We left asking him to take a test the following day."

There was a beat.

Then all hell broke loose in the courtroom.

"Objection, Your Honor!" Schwartz said.

"This is—!" defense attorney Roberto Puentes started to say, getting interrupted by his own co-counsel, Michael Schwartz, who said, "We need to have a little conference outside the presence of the jury at this point."

The judge instantly agreed.

"Ladies and gentlemen," he told the jury, "you'll be excused at this time. During this recess you're instructed not to discuss this case amongst yourselves or with anyone else. You're instructed not to form any opinion of the case, and you are not to read, listen or view any news accounts of the case." The jurors filed out, and the judge said, "The jury is excused. The record should reflect these proceedings are occurring outside the presence of the jury. Mr. Schwartz?"

Schwartz said, "The defense is going to have to move for a mistrial at this point."

The reason was Beltron's reference to "the test."

"Everybody in this courtroom knows that mentioning a polygraph under these circumstances, or a test which clearly could only be a polygraph, is improper," said Schwartz. "It's unlawful. I cannot imagine what anybody would be thinking to produce such testimony, and it simply has to be— There has to be a mistrial. There's just no other alternative at this point."

"Thank you," the judge said. "Briefly, Mr. Clifton."

"I didn't ever instruct this witness to mention a test," said Clifton.

To Beltron, the judge asked sharply, "Why did you mention asking him to take a test?"

"That's how we left at the end of the day. I apologize." The magnitude of what he had just done hit Beltron like a ton of bricks.

"You know, certainly," the judge said, "the law in Nevada about the inadmissibility about polygraph?"

"Yes, sir," the detective said.

"You know we took three days to select a jury. Do you have any idea what it cost the people of the state of Nevada to go through a trial this far?"

"I'm sure it's expensive."

"Why did you refer to a test?"

"That's how we ended the day, sir."

Although he knew that a polygraph should never be mentioned in court, Clifton did note that the defense had a copy of the taped interview of Bergna that had mention of "the test" on it, but that the defense didn't object or edit out that reference.

"Respond to what Mr. Clifton said," the judge told defense attorney Smith. "Did you edit the tape in such a way it mentions the polygraph?"

Smith said there was some miscommunication, that there wasn't just one interview and there wasn't just one tape. There was an audiotape of the first interview and videotape of the next two interviews. The lawyers then argued over who had what tape and what was taken out of what tape and by whom.

"We gave them our copy we were going to use if he didn't want to use his! He said he agreed!" Clifton said.

"Mr. Clifton, will you stop talking about things I didn't say?" said Smith.

"That's not true!"

"Gentlemen, excuse me just a second! Now, be still and listen to me!" the judge snapped. "I've had enough of the lawyers in this trial interrupting each other and making comments, so it will stop now. If it continues, the next person who does it will pay fifty dollars cash the same day. If we do it again, it goes to a hundred, and doubles every time. Then we talk about a contempt hearing. So there will be no more of that during this trial! Period. Now, let me ask this question one more time. Is there a version of the videotape, reviewed and redacted by the defense, that's been shown to the state before the one-thirty proceeding started this afternoon?"

"No, Your Honor, there is not," said Smith.

"OK. All right," the judge said, cooling down. "The motion for mistrial is denied because the only reference so far in the trial has been to a 'test.' Detective Beltron and Mr. Clifton, let me advise you, and Mr. Clifton, let me advise you to instruct other witnesses very, very carefully: If there's any other allusion of any kind to polygraph, there will be a mistrial. Return the jury to the courtroom."

Schwartz wasn't satisfied. "Your Honor, will there be any discussion of how to address the fact that the bell has been rung?"—legalese for "the damage has already been done."

"I think the best way to address it is to do nothing," said the judge. "There's no description what the 'test' is. The court's instruction is not to allude to it directly or indirectly. I think the best thing is not to draw attention to it by reference."

The jury was brought back in, and Beltron resumed his testimony as if none of the fighting had occurred, telling jurors about how the interview was conducted, how Bergna had some minor injuries, how the blood and urine tests turned up minor traces of morphine from the hospital but no alcohol or other drugs.

The case, which had teetered on the brink of mistrial, was back on track, much to the relief of prosecutors and to Beltron.

During his testimony, Clifton played the audiotape of Bergna's first interview with police. The recording was scratchy and barely intelligible much of the time, and jurors followed along on a transcript. But the prosecution was able to very clearly place before the jury what it considered Bergna's many missteps—the two versions of whether his wife was ever up on the mountain, his memory loss at just the moment the truck went over the cliff, his long rambling laments about how his wife's absences left him feeling lonely. All of this Clifton would use in closing statements to contend that Bergna was lying.

Later in the day, after the jury was gone, Clifton sought to make amends. "May the record reflect that this was not intentional," he said. "I think Detective Beltron, or Sergeant Beltron, apologized to the court. I certainly have warned him, as have my investigators. I think he was told three times today alone not to mention the polygraph or the test itself. He is a seasoned veteran. I guess it was just a slip."

The judge was in no mood for apologies. "He's going to be a retired veteran if he even thinks about mentioning anything about it again," Adams said. "If it wasn't intentional, it was the dumbest thing I can imagine. I think the Nevada rule on polygraph is about as well known as Miranda [the reading-your-rights rule]. I mean it. If he says or anybody ever says one more word about tests or a polygraph, then we'll have mistrial, then we'll have an argument about whether the manifest of a retrial or dismissal is appropriate. And if we have a retrial, it starts Monday and if we don't, you all go to the Supreme Court. Well, I said all I wanted to say."

Clifton had more to say. "I want to make a record."

"There's no point trying to save him," the judge said. "He's already drowned. Go on to the next thing."

Later, Beltron would fully admit to his mistake, saying he was concentrating so much on the questions—and answering them accurately—that he was a little too accurate, answering what he shouldn't have. "I wasn't mad at Dave Clifton at all," he would recall months later. "We had gone over it: You can't make any mention of it. I obviously knew it was state law. Unfortunately, I embarrassed myself and the department. It was just one of those things."

The next day, jurors would watch the videotape of Bergna's back-to-back interviews at the Reno sheriff's station, witnessing the increasingly confrontational relationship between Bergna and his inquisitor, Beltron, with Bergna at one point hobbling out of the station in apparent anger and disgust, then returning, chastened, with his father at his side, but never admitting to anything other than making a mistake up on the mountain.

Although the jurors could see Bergna's demeanor for themselves, Clifton elicited from Beltron his own observations.

"Sergeant Beltron, with all the crying you saw on behalf of the defendant, how many times did you hand him a Kleenex?"

"I never did, sir."

"Why not?"

"I didn't have any reason to give him one. He wasn't tearing."

Beltron explained that the second videotaped interview that day hadn't been planned—until he overheard a conversation at the basement elevator between Bergna and his father.

"What was the statement you heard by the defendant?" asked Clifton.

"That 'I did it.' "

"How close in relation were you to the two of them when you heard it?"

"I was near them, less than five feet away."

"Was it unusual enough to you to come back to him in the interview about it?"

"That's why I asked him to have that interview."

The Beltron-bashing didn't stop with the prosecution questioning. During cross-examination, Schwartz sought to show that the police work by Beltron and others was not only shoddy, but done in a way to justify preconceived ideas about Bergna's guilt. Schwartz asked, for instance, if police made any effort to see whether those celebrated missing gas can caps were left at the AM/PM store.

"I think we checked it, but I don't think we found anything," said Beltron.

"Is there any documentation to support that?"

"Not that I'm aware of, sir."

"It seems to have happened a good deal in this case," said Schwartz. "Was there something unusual or unique about this case that caused people not to create documentation, not to put into writing what they were doing, what they were doing and what they were learning?"

Clifton objected, and the judge sustained the objection.

Schwartz then tried to show that Bergna's answers during the interviews couldn't be trusted.

"Deputy," Schwartz said, giving the sergeant a demotion, "isn't it true that Mr. Bergna constantly agreed with things that actually weren't true simply because you said them?"

"He said, 'If you say so' a lot."

"OK, but didn't he also agree with you on other things, actually agree with you on a number of matters that actually weren't true?"

"Yes."

"OK, did you or do you now have any concern at all about the veracity, the legitimacy of this interrogation of Mr. Bergna?"

"He answered my questions, and he agreed with some of them and disagreed with others."

The lawyer suggested that Bergna was fatigued.

"So he was being interviewed for over six hours on June second, correct?"

"Yes, sir."

"In addition to the two hours that he was interviewed on June first?"

"Yes, sir."

"All right, after his wife has died a horrible death, right?"

"Yes, sir."

"And you had no concern for his state of mind during this interrogation process? Is that your testimony?"

"We asked him repeatedly if he wanted something to drink, if he was comfortable."

"And that was good enough for you?"

"In my opinion, yes."

The cross-examination of Beltron went into another day, Friday, October 12, 2001, as Schwartz continued to insist that Bergna was railroaded.

"Is it by design or coincidence that the things that

you ultimately chose to believe somehow support your theory of intentional murder, and the things that you chose not to believe tend to indicate that Mr. Bergna is innocent?"

"I don't understand."

"Well, anything that might have contradicted your theory . . . you decided was either untrue or impossible, right?"

"You'd have to give me a specific thing. I don't know exactly what it is. I mean, he didn't lie about everything. He admitted to being there."

Schwartz then threw a big curve. He challenged Beltron on the detective's suggestion that Bergna's memory lapses about key events during the accident were somehow suspicious.

"In light of the fact that you found Mr. Bergna's inability to remember or explain an indication of lack of candor, how exactly is it that you explain the fact that when *you* killed someone in a motor vehicle accident, you couldn't remember everything?"

Clifton sprang to his feet. "Your Honor, maybe we'd better approach. That was unbelievable."

The lawyers had a discussion at the bench, after which the judge said, "You may answer the question."

It turned out that during a January 1986 police pursuit by Beltron of a person driving in the wrong lane, that person was killed when he veered in front of Beltron's squad car. During the follow-up investigation of that crash, Beltron had incorrectly recalled some of the facts, including the speed of the pursuit.

"There are some things I can't remember from the accident because of the close proximities, displacement of things," acknowledged Beltron.

"And that's normal, isn't it?" asked Schwartz.

"Yes."

"You didn't intend to hurt anyone in that accident, did you?"

"No, sir."

"Isn't it at least possible that Peter Bergna didn't intend to hurt anybody in this case?"

Beltron, battered as he was, didn't take the bait. "No, sir."

Chapter 34

Over the next few days the tone of the trial would settle down, as the prosecution shifted the focus to the physical evidence, eliciting testimony about the gas cans with the missing cap pieces and the asphalt stains on Bergna's shoes and clothes. The scientist who examined the cornstarch on the clothes came in to say he found amounts consistent with what would be flying around in the air anyway. The coroner testified that Rinette appeared to die from the massive injuries from the car crash and couldn't say whether she was killed by any means before the crash. And the highway patrol mechanic testified that the brakes on the truck appeared to be in working order.

From there, the prosecution moved to the issue of the motive, calling Karen Owen, Joan Dunklee and Maxine Preston to recount how Bergna told them at the principal's retirement party how lonely he was with Rinette in Europe. For the most part, the defense didn't challenge the women's testimony, though attorney David Smith suggested that Owen had a petty score to settle with Bergna.

He asked her if she was aware that Bergna had called the animal control authorities about her two dogs.

"I don't recall that he'd called animal control," she said, though she did recall a time when her black Labrador puppy had destroyed some of Mrs. Bergna's tulips and "Mr. Bergna may have come over to talk about it."

Leo Humphreys, the bank executive, testified about how a couple weeks before the accident, Bergna had asked him about Janet Mello and whether she was married. Then Mello came into court and recounted how they had met at the appraisal fair. "He was a stranger to me," she said. Later, after the accident, "He called my office . . . and asked me if I would be interested in going to the movies with him. I said no." Audrey Tedore testified about the surprise birthday party before the accident, and how she asked her friend Brenda to "run interference" to keep Bergna from trying to dance with her at a club. And Brenda Redl-Harge testified about how her relationship with Bergna after the accident reached that uncomfortable night in the hot tub when he touched her breast.

Predictably, Redl-Harge got the sharpest cross-examination of the group, just as she did at the pre-trial hearing. When she said she didn't trust Bergna, defense attorney Roberto Puentes shot back: "So we have this man that you don't trust, makes you nervous, distrustful, yet you put on your bathing suit, got in your car, drove up there knowing you were going to have dinner and hot tub with him. Am I missing something?"

Rinette's boss at the tour agency, Kendra St. John, spoke of Rinette's mid-life career change and how she was prepared to spend more time in Europe, not less. And she testified about Bergna's "inappropriate" actions after the memorial service for Rinette.

Finally, Bergna neighbor Cindy Glatz testified about what she called the increasing number of arguments between Peter and Rinette, leading up to Peter's snow-blower assault on his wife. The cross-examination of Glatz was even fiercer than that of Redl-Harge, as the defense sought to show that she had a vendetta against Bergna.

"Ms. Glatz, you finally got your day in court, right?" asked Puentes.

"This isn't my day in court," she coldly replied.

Puentes sought to portray her as a busybody homemaker neighbor, suggesting she had complained that Bergna had left his Christmas lights up too long and wasn't taking care of his yard.

The emotion in the courtroom intensified when Rinette's brother, Richard Riella, testified. Finally getting to confront Bergna in court now that the family's wrongful death suit had been settled, Riella went over Rinette's life history, the tensions he saw in the marriage between Peter and Rinette—including her travel schedule and refusal to have children—and his own clashes with Peter over Rinette's inheritance.

The delicate matter of cross-examining the still-grieving yet obviously still-bitter brother of Rinette went to defense attorney David Smith, who began with a greeting:

"Good afternoon, Mr. Riella, how are you?"

"Fair."

"Would it be fair to say, sir, that you loved your sister dearly?"

"Yes."

"Would it be fair to say that whether Peter Bergna's convicted or not of murdering Rinette, you will always hold him responsible for her death?"

"Yes."

From there, the cross-examination picked up intensity. Smith grilled Richard on whether there was a dispute in the Riella family over the inheritance—and suggested Peter wasn't the only one with a beef about where the money went. Over prosecution objections Smith asked, "Isn't it true that for approximately six months before Rinette's death she and [brother] John had stopped talking because of an argument they'd had about the handling of the Riella Ranch Partnership?"

"No, that's not true."

"Do you recall a meeting at your house between John, you and Rinette in which you discussed whether or not to include a—call it an aunt, but really was a half-sister of your mother—in one of the family ranches that was purchased with some stock and bonds that were inherited?"

"You're— That's not what the conversation was about."

"OK, do you recall Rinette becoming tearful and upset during this conversation with John?"

"Not tearful."

"Would you be surprised if she told other people that she and John had had a falling out?"

"Yes."

"Because of money about the ranch?"

"They didn't have a falling out. They had a disagreement over a business matter."

"OK."

"That we had a glass of wine on fifteen minutes over with. After it was over."

Smith then went over the partnership agreement in great detail, how the shares would be split, how the property value would be determined, how spouses and their children played in. At several points, Richard Riella said he didn't know the ins and outs of the agreement and the subsequent legal dispute with Peter over it because the agreement was drafted and interpreted by lawyers.

Finally, the judge said, "I think we're just taking too

much time because of the legal gobbledegook in the lawsuit we just discussed."

Smith took another crack at it and got no more out of
Riella than the fact that the brothers settled for $220,000
from Bergna's insurance company. Finally, the judge
said, "Let's move on."

Later, Smith sought to show that Riella had a financial
stake in Bergna's conviction. The lawyer suggested Rick
and his brothers would benefit because Bergna couldn't
inherit property from his wife if convicted of murder. As
Rick continued to plead ignorance about the details of
how this would work, the judge asked finally:

"If he is convicted, will you pursue a civil claim on behalf of the family?"

"I would have to talk it over with my brother. Him and
I would have to agree on it."

"What's your view?"

"If he's found guilty of killing my sister, I don't want
him to have money that my parents worked all their life to
earn."

Smith then challenged the severity and relevance of
the marital spats that Rick witnessed between Peter and
Rinette.

"They argued like couples do about money from time
to time, but aside from that, you thought that Rinette
loved Peter and Peter loved Rinette. Isn't that right?"
asked Smith.

"No, it's not true."

"You argue with your wife?"

"Yes."

Clifton rose and said, "Your Honor, I'd object. We're
getting to comparing marriages again. It's not relevant."

The judge overruled the objection, but told Smith to
move on.

Rick did acknowledge that in a statement to police, he

wrote: "The relationship between Peter and Rinette appeared to be normal other than the fact that my sister, Rinette, enjoyed traveling and was away a considerable amount of time."

"Sir," said Smith, "it hurts you a great deal that your sister died in a motor vehicle that was driven by Peter Bergna, right?"

"Yes."

"That hurt was magnified when the two of you got into a dispute about money, isn't that right?"

"Yes."

"I have no more questions. Thank you."

On redirect examination by Clifton, Rick insisted that he didn't care about money when he sued Bergna or whether he would get any more if he's convicted.

"Is that your main concern at this point?"

"The money?"

"Yes."

"Was never our main concern."

"Is it now?"

"No."

"Will it be if he gets convicted?"

"That is our main concern—to find out why our sister landed up seven hundred feet down a cliff."

"OK, to see justice done?"

"Yes."

Chapter 35

It was in the middle of Richard Riella's testimony that the judge informed the jurors that their information about this 700-foot cliff wasn't just going to be a matter of testimony and photographs. "Tomorrow," Judge Adams told them, "we will convene promptly at ten a.m. here at the courthouse. The jury will then be taken by transport to the site which is the subject of this trial."

Judge Adams had issued the ground rules the day before: wear casual clothes, use the restroom first, show up on time to catch the bus, bring your notepads if you wish. He told them they didn't have to worry about food—the bus would be stopping at Port of Subs for lunch—and they didn't have to worry about the reporters and photographers buzzing around. "All media representatives were strictly instructed not to take any motion or still photographs that disclose the identity of any juror, so no matter where you go on the site or walk around or what you do, nobody will be photographing you, you can be confident," the judge said.

They were driven up Mount Rose, turned left at the Slide Mountain access road, went a couple miles to the dead end at the ski area where Rinette Riella-Bergna spent her final hours discussing her marriage with Peter Bergna. They got out and walked the same pavement that Peter paced with his cigar, then walked down to the turn-out where the Ford F-150 slammed through the guardrail and plunged Rinette to her death. The guardrail had long since been replaced, but three orange highway cones marked the spot where the truck had crashed through.

The only one to speak was Judge Adams. Wearing sunglasses and a sweater, the judge noted for the record that it was 11:22 a.m. and said, "Counsel and defendant are present with court, state and jury on Mount Rose." Next to him, the court reporter had set up her machine on the pavement and tapped in the words. Then, 3,000 feet above the Washoe Valley, there were only the sounds of feet crunching on gravel and winds—winds that on another day would send a hang glider soaring over the ridge. The little group on the mountain—the jurors, the lawyers, the court staff, the reporters and Peter Bergna—milled around, saying nothing. No testimony would be allowed. This was merely a site visit.

Jurors wandered around the area, taking notes. One examined the bolts that fastened the guardrail to the wooden post. Several peered over the sharp drop-off. At one point, Peter—wearing a suit, no shackles, but guarded by nearby sheriff's deputies—walked to the other side of the guardrail and stood, arms down, and peered down the cliff, his attorneys standing a few feet behind him. He looked over the edge to that spot eighty feet below where he'd lain in the dirt and spoken to 911 dispatcher Michelle Lewis and screamed for Rinette. He looked farther down, where there was a yellow flag marking the spot where his blue pickup had come to a rest, upside down, facing up-hill, with Rinette dead inside.

At 11:41 a.m., the judge announced for the record that the site tour had ended.

Chapter 36

Through the month of October 2001, the trial of Peter Bergna had already had its share of drama—the blistering cross-examination of Trooper Schilling, the near-mistrial, the playing of Bergna's taped police interviews, the testimony of women in his life and the victim's angry brother, the visit to the scene of the crash. But now the case was about to take a turn for the tedious as the defense and prosecution planned to put on a parade of expert witnesses who would drone on about the angles and the velocities and the impacts and every other aspect of the analysis of truck metal hitting guardrail metal.

But before the trial got into the realm of physics and engineering, there would be one more piece of intrigue.

It would come from a very nervous man named Darrell Coursey.

Coursey was at the moment a resident of a Nevada prison, beginning a 10- to 25-year term for robbery. Before he was transferred to the prison, he had been incarcerated at the Washoe County Jail, where Peter Bergna also was being held. There, Coursey claimed, he overheard Bergna say something that he thought the authorities would want to hear. But after he reported it, he discovered much to his chagrin that Peter Bergna wasn't just any inmate.

"He had no idea that Peter was somebody who was 'rich and famous,'" said prosecutor Kelli Anne Bell, who was working with Clifton, at a hearing on October 16, 2001, on whether to make special security arrangements for Coursey's testimony. "He feels sort of as a sitting duck in prison. They watch *48 Hours* there and there's going to be a piece on the TV screen. . . . Mr. Bergna has a group of people that he hangs out with. He [Coursey] believes that those people are going to give him bad food while he's in."

Judge Brent Adams wasn't impressed. "My wife's been doing that for two years," he said.

"The point is, all he asks is that his name and face not be shown," said Bell.

"Not shown on TV?"

Yes, Bell said, to which defense attorney Michael Schwartz said, "I don't see why we should be making any special arrangements for this witness."

The judge hauled Coursey into the courtroom to find out just how fearful he really was.

"Well, sir," said Coursey, "I have to do at least ten years in prison before I get parole and I am, with my record, I'm probably going to have to do, you know, fifteen before I get out. . . . The fact of the matter is that putting my name in the newspaper or having me on TV could cause me great damage in prison and also to my family." He had children ages 9, 11 and 13. He said that in jail he had been "called names and, you know, stared at."

Judge Adams *still* wasn't impressed. He ordered that Coursey's testimony would be allowed, and a week after the hearing, on October 22—the Monday after the jury visit to Slide Mountain—Darrell Coursey was back in Adams' court to tell what he'd overheard Peter Bergna say during a Bible study class in jail.

Questioned by Bell, Coursey explained that he had begun attending the 7:30-to-8:30 p.m. classes, led by another inmate named Dave, in the Washoe County Jail's multipurpose room. "He knew a lot about the Bible, so he teaches stuff," he said. "I've been a drug addict and a thief all my life and I've never done anything, really, you know worthily. And I just—it's kind of hard to explain—but it's kind of like you have a spiritual awakening. You just one day wake up and go, 'Man, I don't really want to do this forever.' "

It was at a Bible study class in July that Coursey met Peter Bergna. Coursey didn't know what he was in for. "After Bible study one evening, I was sitting at a table with a couple of individuals and Mr. Bergna and he asked me some questions about prison. He asked me about the prison system, and I told him that they were, you know, pretty much all right except for Ely"—the state prison. "He said that if he was convicted, that's where he would go. He said he was in for killing his wife."

But Bergna would say more than that, according to Coursey.

"He said, 'I killed my wife,' " the inmate said. "Specifically he told me that he drove his truck off the side of a cliff."

"And what did he say he did?" asked Bell.

"Jumped out of the truck. I said that was a pretty neat trick: She just sat in the truck? He goes, 'She was unconscious at the time.' I said, 'You know, so you've changed now. You're going to Bible study.' You know, because you're figuring if you mess up, Bible study would be a cool place to go, I guess. And he said that he had been a Christian on the streets."

"Did he tell you why he committed the murder?"

"He said because his wife didn't want to have children."

"Did you ask him about why he didn't just get a divorce?"

"Yes, ma'am."

"And what did he say?"

"He said there were financial issues."

"And did you ask him to clarify what they were?"

"I don't believe so. He didn't really say, just financial issues."

The prosecutor asked Coursey what Bergna's demeanor was when he was saying these things.

"He was pretty intense."

"Did he strike you as being remorseful?"

Before the judge could rule on a defense objection, Coursey said, "No, ma'am."

And there was something else that Bergna said.

"He said that he had a good attorney and he didn't think that he was going to get convicted."

Coursey said that at this point he didn't know Bergna or anything about him—including the notoriety the case had generated. Coursey went to Deputy Kirk Holden at the jail and told him about the conversation. Coursey had been a snitch for Holden before. He had given police information over the summer about an inmate awaiting sentence on a murder conviction. In exchange, he got a lesser sentence on the robberies. He claimed he got nothing in exchange for coming forward about Bergna, but now was nervous because word would get out among the other inmates due to the high-profile nature of the case.

"I didn't know that this was going to come to anything. And I didn't know at that time that I would have to come and testify and I didn't know that there were going to be news cameras or anything like that," he said. "I talked to some people at my church and my pastor, and they said that I shouldn't keep something in darkness, but bring it to light." He added, "My pastor told me that sometimes it's more difficult to do the right thing." Still, he said, he was scared. "Wherever I go, I'll have to have two deputies with me," he said. "It means I only get an hour out of my cell. It means I won't get visitors. It's like I'm a target."

After he wrapped up his direct testimony, it was time for the cross-examination. Bergna's attorney, Michael Schwartz, listened as this witness gave testimony saying that Bergna had confessed to murder. If the jury believed Coursey, the case was over. Even if the jury half-believed Coursey—and thought that the other evidence backed him up—the case was over. Schwartz went on the attack.

"Thanks for the unsolicited testimony, Mr. Coursey," he snarled. "Or shall we call you by some other name today? Frank Wagen Poogie? Is that a name you've gone by in the past?"

"No, sir, but it does appear on my alias list."

"Darrell Wayne Coursey?"

"No, sir."

"That appears on your alias list?"

"Yes, sir."

"Darren William Cox?"

"Yes, sir, I have used that alias."

"Danell Carsey?"

"No, sir."

"You haven't used that one?"

"No, sir."

"Thomas Basco?"

"Tom Basco. Yes, sir, I used that one."

And on the names went: Darrell Corely, Darrell Cox, James North, Danell Carsey Jr., Darrell Tomas Coursey.

"Randy Smith?"

"Yes, sir."

"Who is Randy W. Smith?"

"It was my wife's brother, sir."

"You used his name?"

"Yes, sir."

"OK."

"Kind of backfired," the witness said. "He had a warrant."

And the courtroom burst into laughter.

But Schwartz wasn't amused. It wasn't enough to discredit Coursey. He had to destroy him. The jury couldn't believe a word the man said. Of course, as a convicted felon, Coursey was extremely vulnerable. Schwartz went through Coursey's long, tangled criminal history, a life filled with crimes and lies—a life as far away from that of an antiques appraiser married to a pharmacist as one could get.

"Now," said Schwartz, "of all the people in the world, you know, however many billion people there are in the world, why do you suppose it is that Mr. Bergna chose you, of all these other people in the world, to confide in, and to say that he had killed his wife? Why do you suppose that is?"

"I have no idea," Coursey said.

"Well, neither do I, which is why I'm asking you. Can you think of any reason?"

"No, sir."

Darrell Coursey left the witness stand and got a one-way ride back to prison, where, if he suffered any reprisals for his testimony, nobody said anything about it during the trial.

It was on this note that the prosecution wound down its

case against Bergna, with only one witness remaining: Rinette's cousin, Gianna Riella, of Lake Como, Italy, who told the jury about how Rinette had had plans to return to Italy, perhaps for a long, long time, as she'd considered buying a condominium under construction. "She was," said Gianna, "very happy." Her testimony was important, though jurors would have to make big inferences—that somehow Peter had heard about these plans of Rinette's to stay in Italy, and thus got even more upset.

But like so much of the case, it was hardly blockbuster evidence. As a circumstantial case, it relied upon the inference, for this and everything else that the prosecution put on. And it relied upon how the jury would view Bergna's own statements to police—his explanations and his demeanor. Peter Bergna was still the key witness of the prosecution case; if the jury didn't believe him, the prosecution wins.

If not, there was an expanse of reasonable doubt as big as the view of the Washoe Valley from Slide Mountain. And as everyone in the courtroom expected, it was that doubt that the defense was about to raise. The only pressing question was whether Peter Bergna was going to take the stand.

Chapter 37

The defense opened its case the same day that Coursey testified by attempting to challenge the validity of the testimony by those women who'd said Peter had hit on them. Lawyers called Teresa Flores, Peter's longtime friend—and the surprise birthday party friend of Brenda Redl-Harge—to try to put a different spin on Peter's behavior after the crash, at least as it related to women. Flores recounted the same Fourth of July picnic at Lake Tahoe that Brenda had mentioned in her testimony, only she painted a much different picture of the romantic dynamics. Flores said there was a very good reason why Bergna watched Brenda's daughter. "I was very embarrassed by Brenda's behavior that day," she said. "She got extremely drunk, had her child [and] totally ignored her, and left her with Peter Bergna while she was on the boat," said Flores. "I was told when she got back, she went topless on the boat and later on that evening she made out on the beach with someone she met earlier that day." Flores portrayed Brenda as the one who'd chased Peter—not the other way around.

Under cross-examination, Flores acknowledged she was still friends with Peter, still sending him cards, and that when Rinette was alive, Flores went to dinner and lunch with him, but never with Rinette. "He found me attractive," she said. "He would boost me when I was down. He would tell me that I had a lot going for me, my personality, my looks, my education, my accomplishments at work."

From there, the defense case shifted, abruptly, from affairs of the heart to the heart of the defense: that Peter Begna's pickup truck had not sailed off the mountain the way the prosecution said it had—hitting the railing at a near–right angle just after Peter bailed out on the pavement. Rather, the defense sought to bolster the theory that the truck skidded along the guardrail, struck a support post, then went into the air in a spinning motion, flinging Bergna out somewhere high up the hill, before the truck went crashing down. This theory was vital to the defense because it would explain why Bergna was left only about eighty feet down the hill, while the truck was down much farther.

On Tuesday, October 23, 2001, the first of many defense experts, Lindley Manning, a consulting mechanical engineer specializing in forensic engineering, took the stand to contradict the prosecution theory. Manning testified that his calculations showed that the truck ran right along the guardrail. "That angle of approach had to be with the truck very nearly parallel to the guardrail, probably something in the order of ten degrees plus or minus a couple," he said. He said that among the evidence of this were scratches on the side of the truck. "The striations of the paint appear to be parallel to the guardrail, and so something was sliding along nearly parallel to make those at an angle of a few degrees," he said. "Sixty degrees seems out of the question."

The defense effort to show that the brakes could have failed was a bust. The defense's own expert, William Rosenbluth, an engineer, examined the truck wreckage and said there was a possibility that the brakes could have gone out, but he wasn't sure. "I couldn't test the brake system on this car," he said. "It was too damaged."

Whether the brakes had failed or not, the defense would contend, the fact was, the guardrail should have stopped the truck. Lowell Shifley Jr., a road-design expert engineer from Reno, testified that a faulty guardrail and substandard maintenance—not a lonely and angry husband—were to blame for the crash. "This guardrail failed because it had missing bolts," he said. "In my opinion, the vehicle should have been re-directed onto the road [by the guardrail] and no one should have been seriously injured, or died." And that wasn't the only problem he found. Shifley said he made fourteen visits to the road and found many defects in maintenance and design. "There aren't any longitudinal white lines and this area is a wide section of pavement," he said. "It's very easy for a driver to get disoriented on a wide section of pavement." He said the guardrail was missing the reflectors, and some wooden posts were leaning, compromising the strength. Also, the double-yellow line was not freshly painted and the road's tilt at the curve was not to specification. "It's unsafe," he said of the road, built in 1952. "It shows a lack of inspection and maintenance." The defense then admitted into evidence a letter from the Nevada Department of Transportation explaining that maintenance was dropped because of the road's short length and lack of traffic. Under cross-examination by Prosecutor Clifton, Shifley acknowledged that, despite the problems with the old, unkept road, "The guardrail didn't cause the crash."

The last of the initial batch of experts, Robert D. Keppel, managing director of Major Case Solutions for

iXP Corp. and an expert in determining whether a crime
scene has been staged, testified on October 24, 2001, that
this accident scene was the real deal. "The characteristics
of this case just don't fit any of the previous two hundred or so staged scenes that I've seen over my career,"
he said. He conceded that the "actions of the defendant
are probably suspicious at best," but not those of somebody "who would have to go out and kill his wife at all."
He said Bergna didn't have a girlfriend or mistress on
the side, and that he didn't take out an insurance policy
close to the time of the accident. Also, it made no sense
for him to jump out of the truck at the last minute—
a highly dangerous maneuver. "He would not risk
his life that way to kill," he said. Keppel said that while
Bergna's actions could have been slightly suspicious,
the police investigation was a disgrace. "I've looked
over thousands of police investigations, and I was shocked
that this one wasn't better documented," he said. "I was
extremely disappointed to see the parade of [investiga-
tors] going over the hillside in the same place the killer
would go. That's basic 101 homicide investigation." He
faulted police for failing to go with Bergna to the hospital and taking all of his clothing as evidence. During
cross-examination by Clifton, Keppel was asked about
the two gas cans in the back of the pickup with the bad
caps. "I admit to you, it's stupid. That's for sure," he
said.

After the experts, the defense brought back witnesses
who were friends of Bergna's, calling soccer coach Mark
Steven Sampson, who described how Peter and Rinette had
what he characterized as usual marital disagreements—in
this case over her travel, her refusal to have children, her
shoddy finances. But, he said, other than that, they
seemed pretty happy. "They joked, they were friendly towards each other, they were loving towards each other,

they bantered, they had enjoyed each other's company," he said. Even though Peter did occasionally flirt with other women—sometimes even in front of Rinette—his wife never seemed to mind. "She would often laugh and just say, 'Well, that's Peter.' But it didn't seem to bother her at all." As for the gas cans in the back of the truck, he said, "He would hunt around, literally for hours, just trying to seek out the cheapest gas he could find. So it's not unusual to me that there were gas cans in his car." Another friend, Gary Espinosa, talked about how Peter helped get the medication for his daughter to battle Tourette syndrome, and how Peter always bragged about "my wife, the doctor." He also said, "Rinette required very little sleep," the inference being that it wouldn't be unheard of for her to accompany Peter up the mountain after a long flight rather than just go home and go to bed. "She was raised on a large cattle ranch, so was an early riser," he said. "She was a person who required about three to four hours of sleep."

The next day, the defense called Bergna's employee, Adelaide Gramanz, to shed some light on his personality— how he liked to get garage sale deals and how, despite his pride in his wine collection, he was not much of a connoisseur—as evidenced by the bad investment in the spoiled wine from the casino. She also spoke of how Rinette's Italy trip caught Peter by surprise and how he didn't like to be alone. She also was used by the defense to try to defuse some of Kendra St. John's testimony about how Bergna seemed too friendly with her the day of the memorial service. "He's just kind of touchy-feely," said Gramanz. "That's how he is, and some people aren't used to that. I'm personally not really that used to it." As for the hot tub incident, "I think he was really lonely," she said. "Most of his friends at Incline were married with kids and so they're pretty involved in a lot of things, and a lot of them weren't around that much . . . also, I think Peter's family is in the Bay Area. He was just lonely."

From the friends' testimony, the defense bounced back to the experts, calling, on October 29, Kay Sweeney, a forensic scientist from Kirkland, Washington, to rebut the prosecution's suggestion that the cornstarch on Bergna's clothing didn't necessarily come from the airbag. "Cornstarch is not that common," she said. "If you find it routinely, something is going on. There's contamination . . . that maybe we need to identify."

Sweeney was followed by Dean Jacobson, a retired Arizona State University material science professor, who said he believed Bergna had been thrown from the pickup's open driver's-side window as it plunged down the cliff. He cited the marks on Bergna's shoes, jacket and pants and a bent piece of molding on the driver's-side window as proof he was ejected from the truck *after* it had broken through the guardrail. "The damage I saw was consistent with Mr. Bergna going head first [out the window]," Jacobson said. "The bottom of these shoes didn't strike anything hard." Using a poster board, Schwartz and Jacobson calculated for the jury the time, speed and force it would have taken for Bergna to open his door, slide across the seat, jump out and then close the door in the crash. It simply would have been impossible, said Jacobson. But during cross-examination, Clifton suggested that Jacobson's calculations didn't match physical evidence at the scene, didn't use correct measurements of the truck and generally "defied the laws of physics." Jacobson relied on a truck speed of 30 mph for his calculations; but earlier testimony by defense experts estimated the speed at between 18 and 20 mph. Jacobson said that much of the information given to him for his calculations came from other defense experts, and he didn't check the accuracy. Jacobson also had no explanation for why the truck hadn't left skid marks on the roadway or paint on the guardrail.

The defense wound down its case by turning up the emotional volume, calling Bergna's brother-in-law, Gerald Quilici, who was married to Peter's sister, to describe a dazed and battered Peter at the funeral for Rinette in Manteca. "He went up to the casket, he knelt down for several minutes and when he got up, he was like in a daze, almost like he was in shock," said Quilici. "He was much more affected by Rinette's death. It was like he was just barely functioning."

Then the defense called Bergna's widowed mother Patricia Bergna, who fought back tears as she told the jury that she had never seen her son fight with Rinette when they spent time with the couple traveling and celebrating holidays. "We wouldn't have taken all those trips with them if we hadn't really enjoyed their company," she said. "They were willing to do everything, try everything."

She also said her son never seemed preoccupied with money.

"It's sort of a mawkish subject, but the estate that you currently possess, what's its value?" asked defense attorney Schwartz.

"It's probably over six million dollars."

"And the plan is, that will by inherited by your four children?"

"Yes, we've already started giving them some at Christmastime. We either give them money or stock."

"OK."

"We're encouraging them to save it for the future generations," said Patricia. "That's how we acquired it, through inheritance, and just saving it."

She then recalled the days surrounding the crash.

"You heard that Rinette died in the accident, right?" asked Schwartz.

"Yes."

"When you heard that, what did you do?"

"Cried."

"That was very painful for you?"

"Yes."

"You two were very close?"

"Yes," she said, breaking up.

"Want to take a moment? You OK?"

She said she was.

At the defense table, Peter was now weeping.

Patricia continued on, saying that her son did the best he could after the crash with a house full of friends and family. She also spoke of how her family felt a chill from Rinette's family at the funeral in Manteca, but that Peter, again, tried to do the best he could.

"In all the time that you saw Peter in the days and weeks and months after Rinette's death, was there any doubt in your mind at all that Peter's sense of loss, his grief, his emotions were sincere and honest?" asked Schwartz.

"There was never any doubt, ever."

In a gentle cross-examination, Clifton sought to show that she was just feeling—and testifying—as any loving mother would.

"Mrs. Bergna, it's fair to say you love your son, correct?"

"Yes."

"You love your other [two] daughters and son, correct?"

"Yes."

"You wouldn't do anything to hurt them, would you?"

"No."

"You wouldn't want to see Mr. Bergna, Peter Bergna, hurt in any way, would you?"

"No."

Clifton also asked her about the inheritance. "I think it was obvious that he's going to inherit money from us. He knew the value of our house. He knew we gave them stocks and money. He knew that they were going to inherit money."

"But at the time of Rinette's death," he asked, "both you and your husband were alive and healthy, correct?"

"Yes."

The last of the defense witnesses included Bergna's neighbor Allan Walker, who spoke of how Peter seemed perfectly normal just hours before the accident—and extremely upset afterwards—but he acknowledged he was a little taken aback by Bergna's amorous escapade in the hot tub: "Perhaps quicker than I would be doing something like that," he said. The prosecution also used Walker to bolster its own case. In a semi-devious line of questioning, Clifton had Walker discuss how gregarious Bergna could be.

"So a Bible study or a church study type group, you would think he would strike up conversation?" asked Clifton, making no mention of inmate snitch Darrell Coursey.

"Yes," said Walker.

The final witness of the defense case was Ronald Wright, Bergna's friend and insurance broker, called to poke holes in the motive claims by telling the jury how it was Rinette's idea to keep the life insurance at $250,000 and his—Wright's—idea to add the $200,000 in accidental death coverage, not Peter's. Wright said that Peter actually wanted to lower the life insurance to $50,000 to $100,000 to save money. He also said that Peter appeared surprised when the $472,596.07 check arrived, because he had forgotten about the accidental death coverage.

But what got to Wright was that the police never asked him about any of this.

"Did you find that surprising?" asked Schwartz.

"I found it ridiculous."

And that was it. The defense rested without calling Peter Bergna to the stand.

Chapter 38

In calling the string of experts to testify, the defense had not only wanted to knock down the prosecution theory of the crash, but to provide support for its alternative scenario, one that would explain how Peter had left the truck and ended up where he did on the mountain with the injuries that he did—and didn't—have. This tactic may have helped provide answers to what the defense attorneys clearly believed were important questions in jurors' minds, but it came at a cost. It turned the tables on the defense. Now the prosecution could poke holes in the defense case, raising reasonable doubts about Bergna's claims of reasonable doubt.

After the defense rested, the prosecution on Thursday, November 8, called a rebuttal witness, Robert H. Turner, a retired University of Nevada, Reno, mechanical engineering professor, to evaluate the mathematical theories that had gone into making the defense's animated recreation of the crash. As the jury chuckled at his folksy remarks, Turner said the video was "shot through with mistakes" and an example of "junk science"—that it would have taken "divine intervention" for the truck to change direction at the guardrail post as dramatically as the defense claimed it did.

"If a junior-level student made this report, I would assign it a 'D,'" the gray-bearded professor said. "After I bled on it with my red pen, I would say you are just all wrong."

Turner also vouched for the credibility of Trooper John Schilling, who had been blasted by a defense expert as "uneducated." "He properly applied the physics equations," Turner said. "I conducted independent calculations and came up with the same results."

After testimony on this mathematical note, Judge Adams announced that summations would be held the following Tuesday and urged jurors to take advantage of the long weekend to relax and get away from the case. "This has been a very long trial and from what I've seen, you have been extremely attentive," he said. "This will be a nice time to rest yourselves."

As it turned out, the jury would need all the rest it could get.

Chapter 39

"For six weeks you've been given two complete contrasting versions of how this happened," Chief Deputy District Attorney Dave Clifton told the jurors on November 13, 2001. "One tells you Mr. Bergna deliberately jumped out of his truck, sending his wife to her death. The other theory is that it was part of a tragic accident which just coincidentally occurred just after they argued over their marital problems and further discussed divorce." The prosecution summation called on jurors to use common sense, to reject far-fetched coincidences and embrace sensible inferences. Clifton noted that only two people were witness to the crash: one was dead, the other sat silently at the defense table as Clifton strolled in front of the jury, showing a picture of a vivacious woman killed just as she'd entered a new, exciting chapter of her life. "Ladies and gentlemen, Rinette Riella-Bergna did nothing, nothing to suffer this demise," said Clifton. "Mr. Bergna murdered his wife."

To persuade jurors to accept the circumstantial case,

Clifton sought to show the folly in the defense theory: that Bergna was flung through the truck's open driver's-side window as the truck barreled through the guardrail. The defense had done more than poke holes in the prosecution case—it presented an alternative scenario of what had happened. And Clifton, the prosecutor, played Clifton, the defense attorney, in summations, as he tried to dismantle Bergna's case. The experts, Clifton claimed, contradicted not only each other, but Bergna himself. Bergna told police he had driven the truck straight toward the guardrail; the defense-hired experts had said Bergna drove alongside the guardrail. Nobody could agree on how fast the truck was going. And nobody could explain why the brakes didn't work. "You are to believe that the brakes, both front and back, failed," Clifton said. "No one found any evidence of any failure."

The prosecution theory, on the other hand, told a logical story supported by the evidence, Clifton said. Zooming in on a picture of Bergna's face taken shortly after the crash, the prosecutor invited jurors to look for the kinds of injuries a person would logically suffer if he was thrown out of a twisting, turning, flying truck onto the side of a steep mountain slope. "The defendant is found with no injuries to his face or neck," Clifton said. "No injuries at all after being ejected head first down a steep embankment filled with gravel. There isn't a scratch."

In murder cases, prosecutors don't have to prove a motive—just that the defendant committed the crime. But few prosecuting attorneys will try a murder case without answering the question of why, even if they themselves are not sure. Before the trial, Clifton privately struggled with a motive. For a time, he considered arguing that Bergna had a murder-suicide planned but chickened out at the last minute. But there wasn't any evidence to support that. In the end, Clifton reasoned that he would take what Bergna himself said at face value. "You have a major, major wedge brewing in their marriage, and he decides to do something about it," Clifton told jurors. "He was obsessed with loneliness. You can see his plan coming into effect." Prosecutors do have to prove premeditation—and thus the reference to the plan, a plan, he said, that began when Bergna picked up Rinette from the airport and drove her up Mount Rose in the middle of the night to the remote dead-end, a list of eleven ways to improve their marriage tucked in his clothing. "He gives her one last ultimatum up there on that hill, when all she wants to do is sleep," said Clifton. "She could have said, 'I'm too tired,' and put her head up against the window and gone to sleep."

But she didn't, and Bergna eliminated her, before looking for someone new—a banker, perhaps, whom he invited into his hot tub. She rebuffed him, but ultimately somebody did not. Four months after her death, Bergna met his fiancée, Robin Russell, and "he had his life back." As for Rinette, he said, "Her death was the only way he could see to get on with his life economically and emotionally. That's how cold-blooded this murder was."

As he appeared before the jury in the final effort to spare Peter Bergna from a lifetime in prison, defense attorney Michael Schwartz countered the prosecution's plea to the jury to connect the dots in this circumstantial case by urging the panel to look for lapses in logic. "A man got into a traffic accident and now he faces the possibility of losing the rest of his life because someone decides to believe something despite the facts of the case," said Schwartz, who led jurors through the evidence, and, with a red marker on a board, checked off what he called each example of reasonable doubt, as he sought to show that the prosecution did not prove to its legal burden that Bergna

jumped from the truck and let it sail off the cliff with
Rinette inside. The clothes, the shoes, the injuries, the
scrapes to the side of the truck—none of it provided sufficient evidence of anything but a terrible accident; all of
it provided a mountain of doubt. "If you have a reason for
that doubt," said Schwartz, "Mr. Bergna is innocent."
Even if a juror had mixed feeling, he said, "then that is a
textbook example of reasonable doubt."

Schwartz then returned to Clifton's remarks, about
how Bergna got his life back through murder, and turned
it upside down. There was no coherent motive shown, the
attorney said. Money? Peter didn't need it. Love after the
crash? That's just life. "Mr. Clifton would have you convict him of murder because Mr. Bergna was lucky enough
to fall in love again," Schwartz said. "Peter's future is
now up to you to spare it, to put it back to where it is supposed to be. You cannot convict him of murder because
you don't like the way he grieved. Give him back his
life."

Chapter 40

The jury had barely begun deliberations when the first sign of trouble arose. On Wednesday, November 14, the day after summations, the jury sent a note to the judge:

> *A juror has used a note in deliberations that he admitted writing at home about the evidence.*

Judge Adams held a closed-door hearing. He tried not to overreact. "My inclination would be, counsel, that we simply have the clerk lodge this in the record of the action," he said. "I don't think there needs to be any response. Do you agree?"

"Yes," defense attorney Schwartz said.

"Yes," prosecutor Clifton said.

"So ordered," said the judge.

Then, the next day, another note came to the judge:

Dear judge,
we are at a stand still. The vote we have taken is
nine to three and no one is willing to budge. We feel
we are in need of you guidance at this point.
Please advise us of what to do now.
                                        Your jury

The panel had been out just two days and it was already deadlocked. The note didn't say which way the jury was leaning, toward guilt or innocence.

Judge Adams held another closed-door chambers meeting. He suggested that the jury be brought into the courtroom and re-read a directive they had heard before beginning deliberation, named Instruction 30, about their duty to deliberate, then tell them to go back into the jury room and go back to work. The attorneys agreed, and the jurors—looking weary—took their seats in the box.

"Ladies and gentlemen of the jury," Judge Adams told them, "let me refresh in your minds Instruction Number Thirty: It is your duty as jurors to consult with one another and to deliberate with a view of reaching an agreement if you can do so without violence to your individual judgment. You each must decide the case for yourself, but should do so only after a consideration of the case with your fellow jurors, and you should not hesitate to change an opinion when convinced that it is erroneous.

"However, you shouldn't be influenced to vote in any way on any question submitted to you by the single fact that a majority of the jurors or any of them favor such a decision. In other words, you should not surrender your honest convictions concerning the effect or weight of evidence for the mere purpose of returning a verdict or solely because of the opinion of the other jurors.

"The court instructs the jury to resume deliberations."

. . .

The next day, Friday, another note came, this one from a panelist identified only as Juror No. One:

> *Your honor,*
> *I feel that I need to let you know something one of the jurors told me. "I cannot give a guilty verdict because I couldn't live with myself later if I found out he was innocent." He then got choked up and stated he [Mr. Bergna] would live with his guilt and God would take care of him. I truly believe this is compromising our vote and we will not be able to bring this to a decision.*

It was signed, "Juror No. One" and came with this PS:

> *He also kept stating he will not change his mind.*

From the stirrings of trouble, to a frustrating deadlock, to dissension in the jury room—deliberations were on the brink of collapse. The second potential mistrial of the case loomed. The proposed remedy from the defense camp was that the jurors, sent home each night to any number of possible distractions and poisonous influences, from media reports to meddlesome neighbors wanting the real scoop on deliberations, should be locked down each night in a hotel until the case was decided one way or another. Defense attorney David Smith suggested that Juror Number One, by coming forward, was now in "grave danger."

Incredulous, the judge asked Smith: "What you're proposing is way beyond that—that some person or group of people is going to systematically figure out who that juror

may be and then take some sort of unspecified acts to co-
erce the juror and capitulating the other jurors. Is that
what you're saying?"

"I'm saying there is a danger of that," said Smith.
"The only way to address that danger, that risk, is to se-
quester the jury."

"We can put them in a sealed box and protect them
from every danger except starvation and lack of air,"
the judge said, and the message was pure sarcasm. He
rejected sequestration and ordered that deliberations
resume.

But the problems didn't end. The word about Juror
Number One's note did get out. One of the other jurors
told the judge in a hearing that he got home and his wife
said that on television she saw somebody hold up a
note that the jury had sent to the judge. The juror told his
wife not to talk about it. "I was a little shocked they had
it," he said.

After the juror recounted this story, defense attorney
Smith said, "The defense would again renew its motion
that a mistrial be declared."

"Denied," said the judge.

Smith then reminded the judge that the jury had been
deadlocked since noon the previous day.

"That's not correct. The court received a note concerning a split of the jurors, nine to three," he said. It was now
Friday. He told the jury to resume deliberations on Monday.

Monday came and so did more strife. Before deliberations even resumed, the defense brought a motion calling
for a mistrial or sequestration on the grounds of prosecu-
torial misconduct and "highly inflammatory media coverage." Defense attorney Smith accused his adversary Dave

Clifton of making prejudicial and improper comments to the media after Juror Number One came forward. "Mr. Clifton's statements have undoubtedly influenced public opinion, and in all likelihood have a coercive impact on the alleged hold-out juror [or jurors] once they are discovered," the defense said in a written motion. Clifton shot back that he wasn't the only one talking to the media; the defense was giving interviews, too. "There has been no prosecutor misconduct," Clifton said. "This is just a futile and desperate attempt by the defense to make a record with the hope of succeeding on future motions or appeals if there is a unanimous verdict."

In a chambers hearing, the judge brought the tired and frazzled jurors in and asked if anyone had read or heard anything about the case. The foreperson indicated that one juror had, a woman identified as Karin Azevedo.

"Ms. Azevedo, have you seen, read or heard anything about this case since leaving the courthouse on Saturday?" the judge asked her.

"Just heard," she said.

"OK, from whom did you hear something?"

"A friend. Actually it was two different instances."

"Would you just tell me what occurred, please?"

"The first one had stated that they had heard that we had voted eleven to one, and I said, 'I cannot discuss the case.' Second one said that they had heard that there was a possible mistrial because of a letter from a juror. I said, 'I cannot discuss the case.' And that was it."

Satisfied that these incidents didn't pollute the juror's mind, the judge ordered the panel to continue discussing the case, which they did, all day, only to emerge at 6:05 p.m. on November 19 without a verdict after fifty hours of deliberations.

After they were brought into the courtroom, the jurors

were asked by the judge, "Is there any juror who believes that additional deliberation in this case would not be fruitful?"

Four women raised their hands. The judge asked again, and then two more women and two men raised their hands. Eight of the twelve jurors now said they didn't believe further deliberations would help.

"All right, thank you," said Adams, who refused to give up. "And what I'm asking you to do is to resume your deliberations tomorrow morning at nine."

Seeing the frustration in the jurors' faces, the judge tried a pep talk. "As I've commented many times during the trial, you have been an extraordinary jury. You've been very thoughtful, very attentive during the lengthy duration of these proceedings. You've all taken copious notes during the trial and you've each studied the individual instructions which were given to you for use during your jury deliberation process, and now you've deliberated since last Tuesday—I think, the total time in excess of fifty hours. The length of deliberations in this case, although unusual, I think, was warranted by the length and complexity of the proceedings. But only you can decide if and when you've reached the moment when additional deliberations are not likely to yield a verdict, whatever your verdict is.

"So I will ask you to return tomorrow morning and at that point, you may want to continue to deliberate, you may not. That is only for you to decide. If you have any communication with the court concerning whether or not you believe the process has been exhausted, then you may do so through the foreperson. So I'll leave it at that for the evening."

He told them to be in the jury room at 9 a.m. "I would like you to search your hearts and minds and communicate through the foreperson to the bailiff in writing whether you believe additional deliberations in this case are warranted. Thank you again for your jury service in this case. And court is in recess."

The next day, Tuesday, at 10:30 a.m., the judge announced that he had received a note from the jury:

> *Your honor and the court,*
> *we, the jury, feel that continuing deliberations*
> *would not produce a unanimous verdict. We truly*
> *feel that we have worked together to the best of our*
> *ability.*

It was signed, "Your jury," followed by the foreperson's name, and dated 11-20-01.

After reading the note, the judge ordered that the jury be brought in.

"All rise for the jury," the bailiff announced, and the jurors entered.

The judge then said:

"Ladies and gentlemen of the jury, I have received a note from the bailiff which you sent to the court this morning advising the court that you do not believe that additional deliberations in this case would be appropriate, and I do respect your decision."

Judge Adams had given up hope. No more compliments, no more prodding, no more appeals to their hearts and minds and patriotism. The case of the *People* vs. *Peter Bergna*—which had taken two-and-a-half years to get to court, six weeks of testimony, and fifty hours of deliberation—was now over without a resolution.

"I'd like to conclude this trial," the judge said, "with some remarks to you that hearken back to the first day of the trial, which is a little bit hard for any of us to remember, and I think I told you at that time that the best service we could render in this time of crisis and war in which our country is engaged is to perform our duty as citizens, to do our best as citizens."

He said he had just gotten off the phone with a friend who had been to Ground Zero in New York, the site where the World Trade Center once stood, now nothing but twisted steel and rubble, "and it was a very moving experience for him. It's a place which has now become hallowed ground. And he underscored to me the importance of the civil process, the non-violent process that we use in our country as a model for the whole world to resolve disputes."

The judge said that while "the military of our country is engaged in actions in far away places," Americans "are living out the ideals which created our country," in courtrooms like the one that had just seen the Peter Bergna trial.

"This has been the longest and perhaps most difficult trial of my twenty-seven-year career as a lawyer and judge," he continued. "I've never seen a better jury. I never have. You ladies and gentlemen watched the testimony and listened with laser-like intensity throughout this long trial. You listened to a great deal of conflicting, complex and hard-to-understand scientific evidence on both sides of the case. You have deliberated for over fifty hours and for almost a week. You have taken copious notes while the lawyers presented their case, and are concerned about the testimony of the witnesses. The judge has the opportunity to observe the jury, and I observed all of you very closely. Not one person, not one person has made a complaint about the evident hardship that jury service has imposed on you, your jobs, your businesses and your families. Not one person has failed to abide by the court's admonitions to avoid reading and listening to news accounts of this case, which have been ubiquitous and nationwide. Not one of you has asked to be relieved from jury service."

He said that sometimes mistrials are viewed as failures. "The lawyers and the judge think, 'Gee, we did our best. We presented the case to you as best we could and somehow a failure has occurred because an answer hasn't been reached,'" the judge said. "But remember what I told you in the initial instructions and reminded you again of during deliberations: that each of you must decide the case for yourself and that you should reach a verdict if you can do so without violence to your individual conscience." He said it was the process, not the result, that distinguishes the US legal system from others, and that the government always wins as long as justice is done.

He concluded by telling them, "I thank you so much for your jury service in this case. It's been an honor to have you in Department Six. The court declares a mistrial in this case. Court is in recess. The jury is discharged."

By the time he had finished speaking, several jurors were in tears.

Later that day, at a hearing, defense attorney Schwartz asked the judge to release Bergna on bail. Schwartz said that in talking to jurors, the panel was split 9–3 in favor of conviction. He also said the DA's office indicated it would take some time to decide whether to try Bergna again. "Under the circumstances, from the defense point of view, it would seem appropriate to admit Mr. Bergna into bail during this pending period where the district attorney is going to stop, reflect and try and determine whether or not the case will be retried," said Schwartz. Asked by the judge what bail conditions Bergna would be willing to accept, Schwartz said, "virtually anything that the court would be inclined to impose," though noted that Bergna would like to leave Nevada. "Mr. Bergna's home

is in Seattle right now. He would like to go to Seattle."
Schwartz said that Bergna had $500,000 equity in the In-
cline house, which could be put up for bail.

Prosecutor Dave Clifton said, "Certainly, as Mr.
Schwartz has pointed out, the state is making no statement
at this time as to whether we will retry or not. I think the
presumption is that we will. That's how the court must look
at this bail issue." He said that he would wait until after the
upcoming Thanksgiving holiday—"to wait a little bit, to
let emotions cool down"—before discussing the retrial issue at the DA's office. He did say that in light of the 9–3
vote, "We first look at the case as being in no worse position than we were before trial. A nine-to-three vote is still
the majority by far." Therefore, he asked the judge that bail
be denied. "Leave Mr. Bergna in custody," said Clifton.
"We are not asking he languish in jail, but if he is going to
be retried and [if] that is the decision of this office, then we
certainly would vehemently oppose any reduction in bail
whatsoever."

Schwartz noted that the jury had initially voted seven
to five for conviction, then changed to nine to three,
where it stayed. He also said that Bergna's family could
scrape up $100,000 for a cash-only bail if need be. The
judge asked if Bergna's mother, who was in the courtroom, would be willing to be a third-party custodian—
risking her property in Saratoga, or cash, if he jumped
bail—and Schwartz, after whispering to Mrs. Bergna,
said, "Mrs. Bergna would agree to do anything requested
by the court to ensure her son's release." The judge then
ordered her to stand and had her swear that she would be
responsible "for assuring the defendant's appearance at
all further proceedings" and that she could be held in
contempt of court if he doesn't show up.

"Is that a responsibility you're willing to take in this
case?"

"Yes," she said.

"The court finds that bail in this case is appropriate," the judge said, setting bail at $750,000, secured by the $500,000 in equity in Bergna's house in Incline Village and $100,000 in cash, and a $150,000 corporate surety. Bergna's mother was ordered to be the third-party custodian, with the threat of contempt of court if her son skipped. Bergna was ordered to relinquish his passport and was allowed to travel only within Washoe County, Nevada; Saratoga, California, where his mother lived; and Seattle, where he owned his home.

"Mr. Bergna," the judge said, "do you understand each of the conditions I've stated?"

"Yes, I do, sir."

"Do you have any questions about them?"

"No, I do not, sir."

"You understand if you violate any condition of release, the following will occur: First, you may be the subject of other charges. Do you understand that?"

"Yes, sir."

"Second, you're going to place your mother in jeopardy as a third-party custodian. That may result in a jail sentence or fine or both against her. Do you understand?"

"Yes, sir."

"Third, your house in Incline Village will be gone and all other property or assets posted on bond on your behalf will be forfeited. Do you understand that?"

"Yes, sir."

"Thank you."

At 6:30 p.m., on Monday, November 19, 2001—almost one year to the day since his arrest on murder charges—Peter Bergna was released from Washoe County Jail. In front of reporters and news cameras, he embraced fiancée Robin Russell and kissed her on the cheeks, then hugged his mother and cried real tears. "I'm happy to be going home, especially on this Thanksgiving," he told reporters. "This has been a very difficult year for me, and I am looking forward to putting my life back together."

Rinette's family expressed no such relief or joy. A dejected Jack Riella, brother of Rinette, told the media: "We wanted a verdict. This just prolongs the agony a little bit. I still believe this is a winnable case. We knew this was a tough case, and I think the prosecution did a hell of a job. I hope they try it again."

Chapter 41

For the Washoe County District Attorney's Office, the decision on whether to retry Peter Bergna was not that difficult to reach. There were, to be sure, considerations, among them expenditure. A quick calculation at the end of the trial found that the DA had spent $95,000 on experts and other costs, and that didn't include still-outstanding bills and travel expenses. Still, "We are not going to compromise justice because we may not have enough money," DA Dick Gammick was quoted as saying in the *Reno Gazette-Journal*. "That's an issue for the county commissioners, not me."

The other consideration was legal: Having failed to convince three jurors of Bergna's guilt beyond a reasonable doubt, was the DA's office still confident it had a strong enough case against him? A 9-to-3 verdict would win a wrongful death suit in civil court, which has the lower preponderance-of-evidence burden of proof, but in criminal court, where a unanimous verdict is required, it's still a loss. After the mistrial, jurors shed light on the closed-door dynamics of deliberations, and prosecutors liked what they saw. Juror Karin Azevedo, for one, suggested it was three jurors who derailed the process. "A lot of things happened inside that jury room that I just don't understand," she told the local paper. One man had his own ideas and would not consider the evidence. One woman couldn't believe Bergna could have jumped from a truck going 25 mph and therefore had to be innocent. And a third juror cited his religious beliefs for refusing to convict. Gammick offered an even more damning view of the three holdouts: "One juror felt that God would have to deal with Bergna and that gets into religious beliefs, another juror relied on his own experience and made up his mind to black out and cut out all the evidence. The third juror had a former spouse who was a police officer and had a biased opinion," he told the *Gazette-Journal*.

In the end, the DA felt it wasn't the nature of the case, but human nature that cost Washoe County a conviction, and, in this gambling mecca, the chances of winning a second trial looked good—"house odds" as they say in the casino business—and one look at the opulent hotels downtown proved that house odds pay off in the long run.

On Wednesday, November 28, 2001, eleven days after the mistrial was declared, Gammick announced that his office would try Bergna again.

Defense attorney David Smith called the decision "an injustice."

Chapter 42

There are 339,000 people in Washoe County, and it would not be a stretch to assume that the overwhelming majority of them knew something about the Peter Bergna murder case. While the case got spotty national attention, it was a fixture of local TV newscasts and dominated the front page of the *Reno Gazette-Journal* for months. Even those who didn't follow the trial closely were likely familiar with the basic storyline: man gets into heated discussion with his wife about marital problems, wife goes off cliff in truck, man miraculously survives and soon ends up with lots of insurance money and a babe in a hot tub. At risk of being lost in all this were legal abstractions like reasonable doubt and the complicated scientific calculations that made up the core of the defense case. It was for this reason—that the prosecution seemed to have the upper hand in the publicity battle—that for the retrial of Peter Bergna, the defense wanted a change of venue, suggesting Las Vegas, at the other end of the state. In a January 2002 story in the *Gazette-Journal,* defense attorney

Michael Schwartz complained about reporters, "The press that you guys have been responsible for has been so negative. The reporting has been unbalanced and I don't think anybody has made any attempt to analyze the prosecution's case . . . and why it didn't add up." He also complained that the DA's office had been "unfair and unprofessional."

As bitter as Schwartz sounded, he would soon have cause for more frustration. On January 7, 2002, Judge Brent Adams denied the defense request for a change of venue, saying that he first wanted to hear what the potential jurors themselves had to say about publicity. That meant that jury selection would proceed in late winter or early spring in Reno, and Bergna's lawyers needed to be prepared to move forward with the trial in Washoe County. They made their statements to the media accordingly, soon presenting as sympathetic a portrait as possible of the Seattle-residing Bergna, now 49 years old—"He desperately wants to get back to work and get on with his life," one of his lawyers told the *Gazette-Journal*—while also revealing what it called "the new information" that would help clear Bergna.

After the March trial date was put off until May, defense attorneys went public with their strategy, attempting to at least plant some ideas in the minds of potential jurors. The defense would still insist that the truck had hit the guardrail at a shallow angle and then spun over on impact, sending Bergna out the window, but this time the defense claimed to have new ammunition against accident reconstructionist Trooper Schilling to show that his calculations were wrong. More important, the defense would offer an explanation for why the truck went out of control: brake failure.

Although Bergna himself had waffled in the police interview over whether the brakes actually didn't work or whether he was accidentally hitting the accelerator instead of the brake pedal, the defense said it had evidence that the kind of truck Bergna drove, a 1997 Ford F-150 pickup, had in fact a history of brake component failures. Attorney David Smith said the defense found more than 10,000 reports of such failures on that model—and Ford knew all about it. Lead counsel Michael Schwartz would later elaborate, telling the press that in the case of Bergna's truck, it was a problem with the vacuum booster that had caused the brakes to give out. The defense said it had documents to prove this and would call a string of people from Ford to testify, as hostile witnesses if necessary. If the defense strategy worked, Ford Motor Company would be as much on trial in Rinette Riella-Bergna's death as her husband.

On Monday, May 6, the first batch of thirty-one potential jurors was brought into Judge Adams' court for the start of jury selection in the second trial. That same day, Schwartz was on the courthouse steps beating the defense publicity drum, telling reporters that he planned to call a local mechanic who had tested the brakes on Bergna's truck and would verify a problem with the vacuum booster. "Since the last trial, we have verified the brakes were bad," Schwartz said.

Jury selection would last three days, with panelists questioned on everything from their exposure to publicity (most had heard something about the case) to what kind of cars they drove (about half drove Fords). In the end, lawyers picked a five-man, seven-woman jury, and on Friday, May 10, 2002—just a few weeks shy of the four-year anniversary of the crash—attorneys gave opening arguments a second time in Judge Brent Adams' court. The prosecution followed the same script as before, with Chief Deputy District Attorney Dave Clifton telling the jury that Bergna had driven his wife off the cliff and bailed out at the last minute to get out of a bad marriage. "Peter Begna killed his wfe deliberately, maliciously and premeditatively," Clifton said. In the defense summation, Michael Schwartz echoed for the jury the claims he had been making outside of court: "You will see for yourself these brakes failed to work properly," he said. He told the jury about the "thousands of complaints" Ford had gotten about the brake components in the F-150 and "Peter Bergna ended up with one of these trucks."

From there, the prosecution case proceeded as it had in the first trial, with testimony from the rescue workers and others who were shocked at how little injury Bergna had suffered in the crash. The prosecution also again called Nevada Highway Patrol mechanic Dewey Willie, only this time his testimony took on heightened importance because of the defense's new bad-brake claims. Again, Willie insisted "there was no mechanical failure," to the brakes or anything else, in Bergna's pickup, including to the brake vacuum booster. "There were no visible signs of rupture," he said. What's more, he said, the truck could have been stopped by the emergency brake, but he found no evidence it had been used.

From there, it was mostly a re-run of the first prosecution case, highlighted by testimony from the women whom Bergna had hit on and from engineering expert Robert Turner to reject as "junk science" the defense claim that Bergna had been ejected from the truck. Turner said that Bergna had had "plenty of time" to jump out of the truck before it hit the guardrail and that had Bergna been ejected as the defense contended, he should have ended up much farther down the hill—at the point of the truck's first impact—than he did.

Meanwhile, Ford made it clear it would not willingly become a co-defendant in a murder trial, filing a motion to prevent five of its Michigan-based employees from testifying for the defense about the alleged history of brake failures in the F-150. Ford contended in its motion that only a "very few" of the thousands of records the defense possessed even mentioned that model of pickup. "They are inaccurate. The vehicle is safe. The brakes performed as they were designed," company spokeswoman Kathleen Vokes told the media. "It appears it is just a ploy to deflect attention."

The defense case also began much as it did in the first trial, with an expert witness called to counter the prosecution's bail-out-of-the-truck theory by saying that Bergna would have suffered "catastrophic" injuries from the pavement if he had. Rather, crime investigator Kay Sweeney, who had testified at the first trial, said, Bergna left the truck after it got airborne and hit the hill on the way down. She also said the truck paint on the guardrail and scratches on the truck showed that the pickup swiped the rail at a "shallow" angle rather than struck it nearly head-on, as prosecutors claimed. In cross-examination, she acknowledged one problem with her theory: Bergna's low-level injuries also were inconsistent with getting thrown into the side of a mountain. "The lack of injuries to the face is kind of a dilemma," she said.

But this acknowledgment was hardly fatal. It was the kind of thing witnesses, particularly experts delving into the fuzzy world of theory, typically have to admit during cross-examination. Bergna's legal team, however, would suffer a much worse blow the next day—one that threatened to gut the defense.

Chapter 43

Both in his remarks to the media and in opening statements, defense attorney Michael Schwartz had contended he could prove that the make, model and year of truck that Peter Bergna drove was plagued by brake problems. The proof, he claimed, lay in the thousands of Ford safety documents obtained by the defense. But on Wednesday, May 29, 2002, Judge Adams said that he had gone through those documents and found they lacked any relevant connection to Bergna's truck. The judge ruled not only that the jury wouldn't be allowed to see the documents, but that the defense also couldn't call the Ford Motor Company officials to testify about the alleged history of brake problems. The judge left open the possibility that the defense could introduce records of complaints related specifically to the brake vacuum booster—which the defense insisted it would do—but the ruling clearly left the Bergna camp in a legal lurch. It had promised something to the jury that it could not now deliver.

The defense case marched on, with lawyers calling

Peter's friends—Gary Espinosa and Tim Gravett—and his mother to tell the jury about how much Bergna loved Rinette and how devastated he was by her death.

The defense then tried to salvage its bad-brakes case by calling mechanic Terry McCreary, who said that one or more brake parts had failed in the truck. He said he'd examined the brake system and found a "good size leak" in the vacuum booster. His testimony was interrupted by yet another skirmish in the trial when it was disclosed that the morning of McCreary's testimony, prosecution witness Dewey Willie had removed a valve from the vacuum booster, sucked on the booster and put the valve back. Schwartz, telling the judge, "I'm stunned," accused the prosecution of felony evidence tampering, while Deputy District Attorney Kelli Anne Viloria (nee Bell, having gotten married since the last trial) said that it was completely appropriate to touch the evidence, and that defense lawyers were in the room the whole time. No action was taken, and McCreary's testimony resumed.

During cross-examination, McCreary acknowledged that the truck still could have been stopped without the power assist from the booster—"You'd have to press a lot harder," he said—and acknowledged that the crash could have also damaged the brake system.

Things would continue to get worse for the defense. The seemingly innocuous testimony from Bergna's friends and mother opened the door for the prosecution to call an incendiary witness: a Hawaii woman named Rebecca Tillery, Bergna's first wife. She had not testified at the first trial, and the defense vigorously argued that her testimony was irrelevant. But in yet another ruling adverse to the defense, the judge allowed it in on the grounds that it balanced the Peter-is-a-nice-guy testimony. Had the defense not made an issue of Peter's personality, then the prosecution would not have been allowed to call a witness to speak to that issue. The defense did, and now it was stuck with Tillery, who told the jury she had been married to Bergna from 1982 to 1985 and that he was hardly the sweet likeable fellow described by his friends. On the second day of their honeymoon, she said, Bergna went "berserk" because she cooked his hash browns improperly. "I was in shock," she said. "He was going on and on. He was so angry at me." She said that she herself had bought into the nice-guy image of Bergna, but "once the door was closed, I found there was a totally different person." She said, "I was very, very fearful of my physical well-being." She acknowledged under cross-examination that she hadn't mentioned any of this during her divorce proceedings, but explained, "I had been taught that you don't talk negatively about your husband."

Having lost the ability to present a key part of the defense, and seeing the defendant's ex-wife paraded to the witness stand, Bergna's defense team entered closing arguments in the second trial in worse shape than it had been in the first. On Friday, June 14, after a two-month retrial, both sides summed up their cases mostly as they had the first time around, this time with Clifton's prosecution partner Kelli Anne Viloria sharing in the argument honors and Michael Schwartz again arguing for the defense. Schwartz got in his final claim that Fords had bad brakes, but Clifton quickly countered by asking the jury why, then, did Bergna buy two Fords in a row? After she had finished her summation, Viloria claimed that Bergna had called her a "bitch."

Deliberations began the following Monday, with the jury asking to see one piece of evidence: the contract Bergna had been carrying the night of the crash that offered eleven ways to improve their marriage. The jury deliberated a second day, on Tuesday, and then, after another half day of talks, on Wednesday, June 19, 2003, sent the judge a note asking if both decisions—guilt and the degree of guilt—must be unanimous. The judge returned a type-written answer saying that they both did need to be unanimous. Prosecutors Clifton and Viloria felt this could be nothing but good for their side.

The jury soon signaled it had reached a verdict.

Chapter 44

It was 2:30 p.m., and Peter Bergna was shaking his head to say no. One after the other, all twelve jurors polled gave the same response. Bergna was guilty of first-degree murder.

The verdict now delivered, Bergna, who had been free on $750,000 bail, was handcuffed and led out of court to jail.

More than four years had passed since the truck crash, four years and two trials and now a conviction. Clifton said he was ecstatic. Viloria said Rinette deserved this day. Rinette's family said justice had been served.

"Not now," said Michael Schwartz, when asked to comment.

The next day, Bergna was brought back into court, and there were tears—tears that, had he shed them four years ago, might have spared him this moment. At his sentencing hearing, he stood before the jury and read a statement that alluded to the Eagle Scout ethics he was taught by his late father, who died not knowing whether his son would be found innocent or guilty. "No matter if I spend the rest of my life in prison, I will always do the right thing," Bergna said. "I will always do what is good." He told the jury that he would always remember Rinette and, "I will always love her."

Bergna's stunned mother, Patricia, told the jury it was wrong. "I know he's innocent," she said. But Rinette's brother Jack said, "He hurt my family. He hurt his family."

After two hours of additional deliberations, the jury came back with a sentence of 20 years to life in prison for the May 31, 1998, murder. Bergna could have gotten more—life without parole—but for a man of 49 years, this term was the same thing. Unless he won an appeal, and got a third trial, Peter Bergna, who could not bear the loneliness when Rinette was away, would in all likelihood die in prison, alone.

Chapter 45

Formal, final sentencing by Judge Brent Adams would have to wait. There would be another twist that would cause another delay when the defense claimed that one of the jurors had talked about the case to her co-worker and family during the trial deliberations, and smoked marijuana during lunch breaks. Judge Adams set a hearing on the juror misconduct claim for August 2002. The source of the misconduct allegations against the juror, now identified as Nicole Abbott, turned out to be one of Bergna's fellow inmates in Housing Unit 8 of the Washoe County Jail, a Christopher Allen Wood, who, when he was not incarcerated, had been an acquaintance of the juror and who had given her rides home from the courthouse. Wood ended up in jail, where he passed on this information to Bergna, who passed it on to his lawyers, who sought a new trial. There was more than a little irony to the fact that the defense, which had so lambasted a jailhouse snitch in Bergna's first trial, now was seeking a new trial on the shoulders of a man awaiting sentencing for trying to burn down his ex-girlfriend's house.

The judge first brought in juror Abbott, who acknowledged that she knew Wood—she described him as the ne'er-do-well friend of her live-in boyfriend—and said she did, in a decision she now regretted, accept rides home from him during the trial. But she denied talking to him or anybody else about the case and denied smoking marijuana. Rather, she said, it was Wood who was the pest, trying to read newspaper accounts of the trial to her during his (unwanted, she claimed) visits to her apartment. Wood also testified, saying that Abbott did in fact talk about the case and did in fact smoke pot. "Right in the middle of smoking a joint, she'd talk about it," he said, adding that he told this to Bergna in a common area of the jail after Wood was incarcerated for pleading guilty on the arson charge.

The misconduct battle would spill into the next month, September 2002, with the appearance of one more jailhouse snitch, this one a Russell Lee Proffitt, jailed on a misdemeanor domestic battery conviction. Proffitt and Wood were cellmates, and Proffitt suggested that Peter Bergna was behind the whole juror misconduct claim coming forward. According to Proffitt, Wood claimed that Bergna offered him $50,000, among other financial incentives, to share the misconduct allegations with the court. What's more, Wood confided to Proffitt that he made the whole thing up—the juror never did actually talk about the case outside of court and never smoked marijuana with him.

After considering arguments from both sides—Schwartz contended, "I can't imagine anything more serious than a juror lying to the court," and Clifton argued that the defense effort was nothing but "sour grapes"—the judge ruled in late September that Peter Bergna had received a fair trial from an impartial jury and didn't deserve a third trial. Adams found that Abbott had done nothing wrong, and that, when all was said and done, the people of the state of Nevada had proved beyond a reasonable doubt that Bergna was guilty.

A month later, on October 29, 2002, Adams formally imposed the sentence decided upon by the jury: 20 years to life. He also ordered Bergna to pay $281,900 in restitution to Rinette's family. Bergna stood and accepted the sentence without emotion. In the courtroom audience were his mother and his fiancée, Robin Russell, who told reporters later that Peter was innocent and she would never stop fighting for him. Also in the audience were six jurors and several members of Rinette's family, who had driven in from Manteca to see the final event of the trial before Bergna was shipped off to the Ely State Prison.

After a short time in prison, Peter had already earned special privileges—extra time on the phone and a radio in his cell.

While in his new cell as his case sat before the Nevada Supreme Court on appeal, Peter has received cards and pictures from old friends like Rick Martin, who was amazed at Peter's positive attitude, all things considered. Peter, he said, was "trying to make the best of things." There's obviously no use for appraising art and antiques in prison, so Peter, putting his background in education to work, had offered to tutor other inmates in English as a second language. He was doing the best he could and trying to set an example, lessons his father had taught him so long ago.